This publication is the exclusive intellectual property of The EOP Foundation.

Without limiting the rights under copyright reserved below, no part of this publication may be reproduced, stored in or introduced into an electronic retrieval system, or transmitted by any means without the prior written permission of the copyright owner and publisher, The EOP Foundation.

The EOP Foundation can provide training assistance to organizations by conducting a seminar on Federal Budget Policies and Processes. The EOP Foundation has published a case study that allows students to portray the roles of the participants in developing the budget process from implementing a budget at the level of field activity through passage of an appropriations bill on the floor of the House of Representatives. Interested parties should contact The EOP Foundation at:

The EOP Foundation
819 7th Street, N.W.
Washington, D.C. 20001
(202) 833-8940

To the Federal employees
who tirelessly toil
preparing,
redoing,
defending,
and carrying out
Federal budgets.

Contents

Acknowledgments

The Foundation acknowledges current and former employees of the Office of Management and Budget who contributed to the book. Special thanks go to colleagues at the EOP Foundation including Michael O'Bannon and Joe Hezir, as well as Alexander Downs for the design and illustrations of the book.

Introduction

Every year, the federal government goes through a drama of developing the federal budget. This year's drama has been more political and partisan than usual given the extraordinary Impeachment focus in the Congress. Though the processes followed in formulating the budget are rather logical and straightforward. However, the issues are surrounded by political controversy.

The final product is a very detailed plan for the coming fiscal year inclusive of a framework of priorities and projections for the future. Every program in the budget is supported by a constituency that believes the expenditures for that program satisfy a vital need. Every tax dollar comes from someone who would rather decide for him or herself how the money should be spent. Balancing these competing demands is the dilemma faced by the political decision-makers, and the end result of the budget process.

Supporting the politicians who must make these difficult decisions are tens of thousands of people, from the White House and Cabinet departments to Congressional staff. Some prepare budget and program proposals, others review these proposals to make sure they make sense, and still others are involved with carrying out the approved budgets.

The objective of this book is to present usable and relevant information about the budget and the budget process in a straightforward and common sense format. Our intent is to explain clearly the facts about the federal budget without making judgments on the political issues.

The individual chapters in this book are largely self-contained, and can be read in any order depending on the interest of the reader. A general guide to this book is as follows.

> Chapter 1 contains a discussion of the budget big picture - size, major components, and budget trends.
>
> Chapter 2 describes the economic and accounting concepts that are used in constructing and implementing the federal budget. These are important

because federal budget concepts are different from those used in general business accounting.

Chapters 3 and 4 examine the composition of federal receipts and spending in detail, including a discussion of historical trends and current trends and patterns. This information is intended to allow the reader to place current issues into perspective.

Chapter 5 summarizes the federal budget process.

Chapters 6, 7, 8, and 9, describe the federal budget processes in-depth, including the major players, their responsibilities, and the "rules of the game".

Chapter 10 describes the process for development and review of government regulations. Although not as visible as the federal budget, regulations require the expenditure of several hundred billions of dollars annually by citizens, businesses, and state and local governments.

Chapter 11 describes the new procedures for management of Information Technology programs. Tightened management of this critical area is expected to improve government productivity and enhance agency operations.

Chapter 12 describes some of the budgetary opportunities and challenges currently facing the nation.

Chapter 13 is an extensive glossary of terms encountered in the budget process.

An appendix at the back of the book contains a listing of the key laws affecting the budget process.

While this book contains information that is current at the time of its printing, it does not attempt to analyze future policies and options for using projected surpluses or reforming the tax system. Instead, the book provides a foundation for the reader to make judgments on current issues and policies.

This is the third edition of "Understanding the Budget of the United States Government." It is the intent of the EOP Foundation to revise this book annually to incorporate the most recent budget data, changes in the budget process, and changes in priorities of the President and the Congress.

Chapter 1

Overview of the Budget

The United States federal government is a big operation. This should not be surprising. The United States is big – 272 million people (the third most populous nation in the world), a land area of over 3 million square miles, the largest Gross Domestic Product (GDP) of any country, and commercial and political interests throughout the world.

The Budget of the U. S. Government exceeds the total GDP of every other country in the world except for Japan and Germany.

After many years of large deficits, the budget now projects large surpluses under current tax and spending laws. While much of this can be attributed to difficult budget decisions made by the President and the Congress, the surpluses also reflect the fact that economic performance has been better than anticipated.

Spending

In fiscal year 2000 (FY 2000), the federal government is planning to spend $1,766 billion – more than $6,400 for every person in the United States. (Figure 1-1)

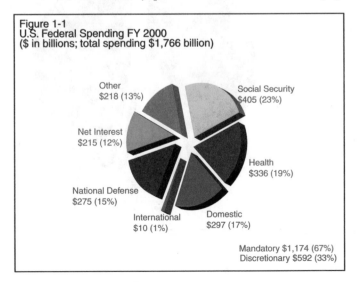

Figure 1-1
U.S. Federal Spending FY 2000
($ in billions; total spending $1,766 billion)

Other $218 (13%)

Social Security $405 (23%)

Net Interest $215 (12%)

Health $336 (19%)

National Defense $275 (15%)

International $10 (1%)

Domestic $297 (17%)

Mandatory $1,174 (67%)
Discretionary $592 (33%)

A growing portion of annual spending is mandatory under current and proposed laws. For FY 2000, this spending totals $1,174 billion and includes:

- $405 billion for Social Security;
- $336 billion for health programs;
- $218 billion for other programs; and
- $215 billion for net interest.

The remaining spending is called discretionary spending and is determined in annual appropriations acts. For FY 2000 this spending is projected at $592 billion and includes:

- $275 billion for national defense;
- $297 billion for domestic programs; and
- $20 billion for international affairs.

Receipts

In FY 2000, receipts are expected to reach $1,883 billion, about $6,800 per person. (Figure 1-2)

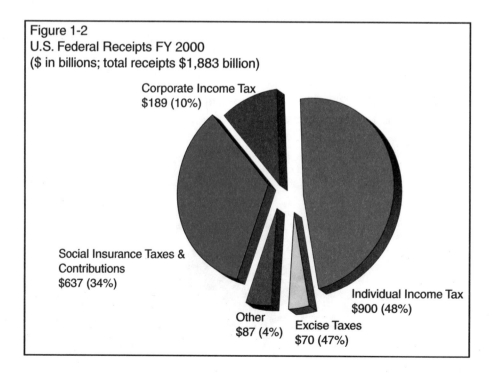

Figure 1-2
U.S. Federal Receipts FY 2000
($ in billions; total receipts $1,883 billion)

Corporate Income Tax
$189 (10%)

Social Insurance Taxes &
Contributions
$637 (34%)

Other
$87 (4%)

Excise Taxes
$70 (47%)

Individual Income Tax
$900 (48%)

Most of these receipts will come for taxes that will continue unless the tax laws are changed. Receipts include:

- $900 billion from individual income taxes;
- $189 billion from corporate income taxes;
- $637 billion from social insurance taxes and contributions including Social Security;
- $70 billion from excise taxes; and
- $87 billion from other taxes and customs duties.

The government also collects fees and service charges, which are treated as offsets to program costs rather than as governmental receipts. Details on fees and service charges are provided in Chapter 3.

Surplus

A budget surplus (receipts greater than spending) of $117 billion is expected for FY 2000.

Spending and Receipts as a Portion of GDP

The FY 2000 budget projects Federal spending at 19.4% of GDP, receipts at 20.7% of GDP.

Spending reached a peacetime high of over 23 percent of GDP in FY 1983. This compares to 19 percent in FY 1970, 18 percent in FY 1960 and 16 percent in FY 1950.

Receipts reached a peacetime high of 20.5 percent of GDP in FY 1968 and a level of 2.6 percent is projected for FY 1999.

The President's Budget projects spending (outlays) declining to 18.1 percent of GDP by 2004. Receipts also would decline as a percent of GDP reaching 20.0 percent in FY 2004.

State and local government spending totals about 9 percent of GDP. In FY 1998, the combined spending of Federal, State and local governments totaled $2,411 billion (28.5 percent of GDP) and receipts totaled $2,624 billion (31.2 percent of GDP). The difference of $213 billion consisted of a Federal surplus of $69 billion and a state and local government surplus of $144 billion.

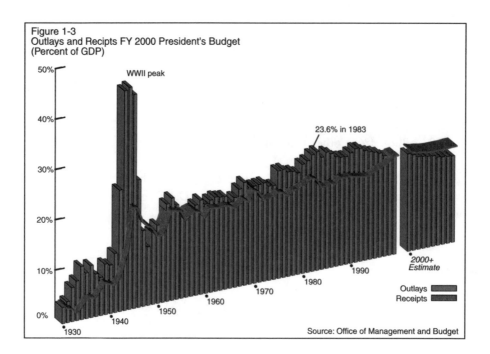

Figure 1-3
Outlays and Recipts FY 2000 President's Budget
(Percent of GDP)

WWII peak

23.6% in 1983

2000+
Estimate

Outlays
Receipts

Source: Office of Management and Budget

Receipts and Spending in Other Countries

Total government spending in the United States consumes a smaller portion of GDP than in most other developed countries. Although direct comparisons of government spending and receipts in the United States with those of other nations can be misleading because the data are not always comparable, such comparisons provide an indication of the role of government in the overall economy.

Spending in other nations tends to exceed that of the United States by large margins. A portion of the difference can be attributed to nationalized health programs in other countries

Japan and Australia are the only major developed nations in which government activities tend to account for about the same percentage of GDP as in the United States. (Table 1-1).

Sensitivity of Budget Estimates to Economic Assumptions

In developing a multi-year budget plan, assumptions must be made about the key economic factors that are anticipated by the budget policies. Those projected in the President's budget for FY 2000 budget are shown in Table 1-2.

4

TABLE 1-1
GENERAL GOVERNMENT RECEIPTS AND SPENDING IN SOME MAJOR INDISTRIALIZED NATIONS IN 1997
(PERCENT OF GDP)

	RECEIPTS	SPENDING	SURPLUS
UNITED STATES	32	32	-
JAPAN	32	35	-3
AUSTRAILIA	35	35	-
UNITED KINGDOM	39	41	-2
CANADA	44	43	1
GERMANY	45	48	-3
ITALY	48	51	-3
FRANCE	51	54	-3
DENMARK	57	56	1
SWEDEN	61	62	-1

SOURCE: ECONOMIC OUTLOOK, DECEMBER 1998, OECD

TABLE 1-2
KEY ECONOMIC ASSUMPTIONS IN THE BUDGET

	1999	2000	2001	2002	2003	2004
REAL GDP GROWTH %	2.0	2.0	2.0	2.4	2.4	2.4
CPI, YEAR OVER YEAR %	2.2	2.3	2.3	2.3	2.3	2.3
UNEMPLOYMENT, AVERAGE ANNUAL %	4.8	5.0	5.3	5.3	5.3	5.3
INTEREST RATES, 10 YEAR TREASURY NOTES %	4.9	5.0	5.2	5.3	5.4	5.4

Projections of receipts and spending are sensitive to the assumptions made about the annual rates of GDP growth, inflation, and interest. A relatively small change over several years in an assumption projected can have a significant impact on future receipts and outlays.

For instance, estimates of real GDP growth one percentage point lower in each of the next five years than the rates assumed in the FY 2000 budget would reduce the projected surplus of $208 billion in 2004 by up to $163 billion. On the other hand, inflation and interest rates one percent higher each year with the real GDP growth assumed in the FY 2000 budget would increase the surplus in FY 2004 by $55 billion. (Table 1-3)

The Imbalance Between Receipts and Spending

Since 1940, deficits have been the rule rather than the exception – 49 years of deficits and only 9 years of surplus.

- The largest deficits occurred in the 1990s.
- In constant (inflation adjusted) dollars, the largest deficits occurred during World War II. The peak was in 1943 when the deficit reached $464 billion in constant 1999 dollars.
- The largest surplus was $69 billion in 1998.

Control on Spending and Receipts

From 1986 through 1997, deficit reduction was the major federal budget issue. Budget projections made in the mid-1980's indicated that annual deficits would exceed $200 billion per year far into the future under the revenue and spending laws in effect at that time.

Several laws were enacted to reduce or eliminate the deficit. These include the Gramm-Rudman-Hollings (GRH) legislation in 1985 and 1987 and the Budget Agreements of 1990, 1993, and 1997. These laws provided for the following:

- revenue increases, i.e., new or higher rates;
- limits on the annual levels of discretionary appropriations;
- a requirement that revenue reductions or mandatory spending increases resulting from new legislation be fully offset by reductions in other mandatory spending or by increases in revenue (Pay-As-You-Go or PAYGO);
- new procedures for Congressional action on the budget; and
- procedures for automatic cuts in spending authority if the estimated deficit or spending levels exceed certain limits.

TABLE 1-3
SENSITIVITY OF BUDGET TO ECONOMIC ASSUMPTIONS
(CHANGE OF ONE PERCENTAGE POINT EACH YEAR (FY 1998-FY 2003))

	CHANGE IN SURPLUS ($ IN BILLIONS)					
	1999	2000	2001	2002	2003	2004
ONE PERCENT LOWER REAL GDP GROWTH (UNEMPLOYMENT 0.5 PERCENTAGE POINT HIGHER)						
RECEIPTS	-8	-25	-46	-68	-92	-118
OUTLAYS	2	8	15	23	33	46
DECREASE IN SURPLUS (-)	-10	-33	-61	-91	-125	-163
ONE PERCENT HIGHER INFLATION AND INTEREST						
RECEIPTS	9	28	47	66	86	109
OUTLAYS	6	19	29	38	46	54
INCREASE IN SURPLUS (+)	4	9	18	28	40	55

SOURCE: THE OFFICE OF MANAGEMENT AND BUDGET

These laws undoubtedly led to smaller deficits than would have occurred otherwise, but they did not result in a balanced budget as required by the GRH legislation in 1985 and 1987 or as projected with the Budget Agreement of 1990. (Figure 1-5)

Despite the tough budget laws, annual budget deficits grew rather than shrunk because actual economic conditions were not as rosy as those assumed in the forecasts. For FY 1995, a surplus of $69 billion was projected to result from the Budget Agreement of 1990, but a deficit of $164 billion actually occurred due in large measure to economic conditions that were worse than those assumed in the agreement.

Changes in economic conditions can cause the deficit to decrease as well as increase. The FY 1998 President's budget released in February 1997 projected a deficit of $125 billion for fiscal year 1997. When the fiscal year ended eight months later, the actual deficit was only $22 billion.

The Budget Agreement of 1997 projected deficits for fiscal years 1999 through 2001; now surpluses are projected. Thus, forecasting is anything but an exact science, and deficit/surplus projections can change substantially in a short period of time.

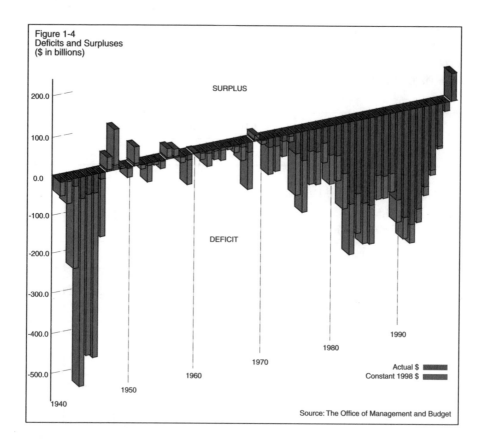

Figure 1-4
Deficits and Surpluses
($ in billions)

SURPLUS

DEFICIT

Actual $
Constant 1998 $

Source: The Office of Management and Budget

The FY 2000 budget recently issued by the President projects surpluses starting in 1998. The Congressional Budget Office (CBO) projects even larger surpluses. (Figure 1-5) The surplus in FY 2004 is projected in the President's Budget at $208 billion and by the CBO at $234 billion under current laws. For the next 15 years, CBO estimates that the surpluses will total nearly $2.6 billion and the Administration projects $2.4 billion, about 10 percent of projected receipts. The principal reason for the differences between CBO and the President's Budget is the choice of economic assumptions.

Although the overall budget will be in a surplus position, there will continue to be deficits in the general fund ($4 billion in 2004), which will be offset by annual surpluses in the Trust Funds ($212 billion in 2004), primarily Social Security, Federal civilian and military retirement, and highways. This is discussed further in Chapter 2.

Federal Debt

The federal debt reflects the cumulative effect of annual deficits.

At the end of FY 1998 (September 1998) the total debt was $5.5 trillion, or more than $20,000 for each person in the United States. This debt included $3.7 trillion held by

8

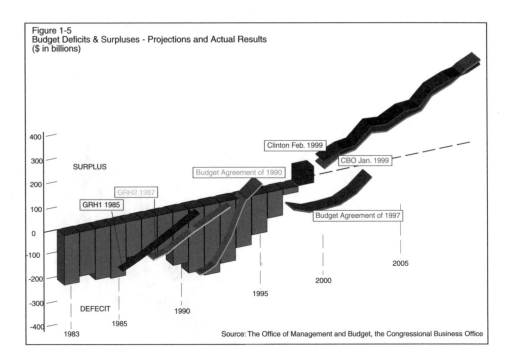

Figure 1-5
Budget Deficits & Surpluses - Projections and Actual Results
($ in billions)

SURPLUS

Clinton Feb. 1999

CBO Jan. 1999

Budget Agreement of 1990

GRH2 1987

GRH1 1985

Budget Agreement of 1997

SURPLUS

DEFECIT

Source: The Office of Management and Budget, the Congressional Business Office

the public and $1.8 trillion held by government accounts, principally the trust funds for Social Security, Medicare, and Federal civilian and military retirement. (Figure 1-6)

The debt held by the public will decline as long as the annual budget is in a surplus position. Total debt will continue to increase, however, reflecting the use of surplus funds in the Trust Funds to cover the cash costs of other government programs.

At the end of FY 1998, the debt held by the public was about 45 percent of GDP, compared to the post World War II low of just under 26 percent in 1981 (Figure 1-7). The President's FY 2000 budget projects the debt dropping to 27 percent of GDP by 2004.

Total governmental debt (Federal, State, and Local government) in the U.S. was about 59 percent of GDP in 1997. Debt to GDP percentages were roughly 60-65 percent in the United Kingdom, Germany and France, and roughly 90 percent in Japan and Canada. (OECD Economic Outlook, December 1998)

Possible Changes to Spending and Receipts

This turnaround in the budget situation has changed the focus of the budget process. Until fall 1997, the focus was on cutting spending to reduce the deficit. The new focus is on what to do with the surpluses.

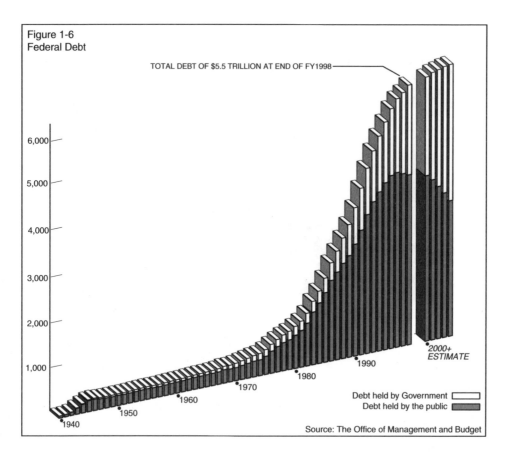

Figure 1-6
Federal Debt

TOTAL DEBT OF $5.5 TRILLION AT END OF FY1998

2000+
ESTIMATE

Debt held by Government
Debt held by the public

Source: The Office of Management and Budget

- The President has proposed that the surpluses be saved to help keep Social Security and Medicare financially viable. The Budget also proposes to use some of the surpluses to pay for increases in discretionary programs.
- Tax cuts and reforms have been proposed by the Congress.
- There is general agreement that spending for certain big priority programs, such as national defense and education, should be increased.

Process reforms likely to be considered include the following:

- Extension of the discretionary budget caps, but at higher levels.
- Biennial budgeting in which funding is appropriated for a two year period rather than one year.

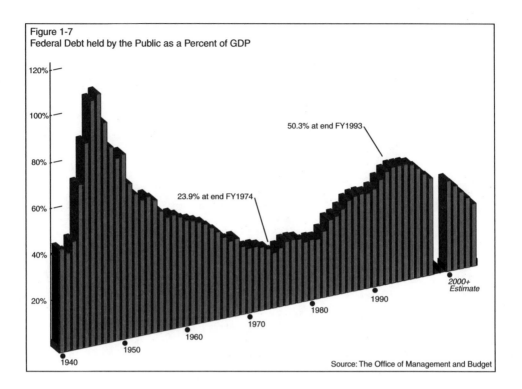

Figure 1-7
Federal Debt held by the Public as a Percent of GDP

50.3% at end FY1993

23.9% at end FY1974

2000+
Estimate

Source: The Office of Management and Budget

11

Chapter 2
Budget Concepts and Rules

There is a lot of jargon associated with the federal budget. Even budgeters get confused over some of the terms. It is little wonder then that budget discussions often are dry and boring. In this book we have tried to limit the use of such vocabulary. Nevertheless, there are some concepts that must be understood to make sense of the budget and the budget process. These "must know" concepts are described in this chapter. A detailed glossary of all the terms that may be found in Chapter 14.

The first point to note is that the government's fiscal year (FY) begins on October 1 of the previous calendar year. That is, FY 1999 began on October 1, 1998, and will end on September 30, 1999.

Budget Authority and Outlays

Budget Authority (BA) is the authority to spend money. It is provided by Congress through legislation and comes in four forms:

- **Appropriation.** This permits obligations to be incurred and payments to be made from government funds.

  Some programs have permanent appropriations and are called direct or mandatory spending programs. Once initiated, these programs never require further appropriations action by the Congress. Unless no money is available for writing government checks, this spending will occur forever. Examples of mandatory spending include Social Security, Medicare, federal government retirement programs, and interest on the federal debt.

  Programs that require annual appropriations are called discretionary spending programs. Funds are provided in thirteen annual appropriations acts. Examples of discretionary programs include national defense and the space program.

- **Borrowing authority.** This permits obligations to be incurred from borrowed funds, usually funds borrowed from the general fund of the Treasury. This is often done for business-type activities that are expected to produce income and repay the borrowed funds with interest.

- **Contract authority**. This permits obligations in advance of an appropriation or in anticipation of receipts that can be used for payment.
- **Spending authority**. This permits obligation of funds received to offset certain program costs, e.g., Medicare, supplementary insurance.

Obligations or commitments by the government to pay for the delivery of goods and services, pay for employees, grants, and subsidies. The government obligates funds when a contract is signed.

Outlays are the payments to settle or liquidate obligations made pursuant to budget authority.

- Unless stated otherwise, the term "spending" refers to outlays.
- Outlays generally reflect cash disbursements. They also include the accrued but unpaid interest on public issues of Treasury debt and cash-equivalent transactions such as the subsidy cost of direct loans and loan guarantees.

Budget authority (BA) provided for a program rarely is fully spent in the year it is made available. Consequently, outlays for a given fiscal year are a result of budget authority provided in the current year and in prior years.

- BA for most major construction and procurement projects covers the entire project cost even though the work and outlays will occur over several years.
- BA for subsidized housing covers contracts that may last up to 40 years.
- BA for most education and job training programs covers school years that do not coincide with federal fiscal years.

The amount of BA carried over from one year to the next and the outlays from prior year BA are substantial. (Table 2-1)

- In FY 2000, about 35 percent of the BA available and 18 percent of the outlays will be from BA provided in prior appropriations acts.
- Only 81 percent of the new BA made available in FY 2000 will be outlaid in FY 2000.

The rate of spending of BA is different for each appropriation account. The Office of Management and Budget (OMB) and the Congressional Budget Office (CBO) each develop spending or outlay rates for every appropriation account. Sometimes the rates are the same, but there is no requirement for agreement. Budget score keepers at OMB and CBO use these outlay rates to estimate the outlays for the President's Budget request and for Congressional legislation.

TABLE 2-1
RELATIONSHIP BETWEEN BUDGET AUTHORITY & OUTLAYS
($ IN BILLIONS)

	BA AVAILABLE IN FY 2000 (%)	OUTLAYS IN FY 2000 (%)	OUTLAYS IN FY 2000 AS A % OF BA AVAILABLE IN FY 2000	OUTLAYS AFTER FY 2000 FROM BA AVAILABLE IN FY 2000
FY 2000 BA	1,781 (65%)	1,445 (82%)	81%	336
PRIOR YEAR BA	950 (35%)	318 (18%)	33%	632
TOTAL	2,731 (100%)	1,763 (100%)	65%	968

SOURCE: THE OFFICE OF MANAGEMENT AND BUDGET

Federal Funds and Trust Funds

Governmental receipts are divided into Federal Fund receipts and Trust Fund receipts. In FY 2000, the President's budget estimates these receipts to be $1,200.7 billion for Federal Funds and $682.3 billion for Trust Funds. (Table 2-2.)

Trust Funds have been established to receive earmarked receipts to carry out specific purposes.

*   Examples include Social Security, Medicare, federal employee retirement, highway construction, and unemployment compensation.
*   The receipts are placed in the Trust Funds and expenditures are made from the Funds. Any unspent funds are invested in treasury securities for which they collect interest. The Trust Funds also receive payments from the Federal Funds to cover the Government's share of Trust Fund Program costs.
*   At the end of FY 1998, the balances in the Trust Funds totaled $1.7 trillion, including Social Security ($730 billion), federal civilian and military retirement ($607 billion), Medicare ($158 billion), and unemployment compensation ($71 billion).

Other receipts and spending are termed Federal Funds.

*   Income tax collections go into the Federal Funds.
*   All borrowing on the national debt is from Federal Funds.

The Federal Funds category has been in a deficit position since 1961 (Figure 2-1).

TABLE 2-2
FEDERAL AND TRUST FUND COLLECTIONS FOR FY 2000 INCLUDED IN THE FY 2000 PRESIDENT'S BUDGET
($ IN BILLIONS)

	FEDERAL FUNDS	TRUST FUNDS	TOTAL
INDIVIDUAL INCOME TAXES	899.7		899.7
CORPORATION INCOMES TAXES	188.1	1.2*	189.4
SOCIAL INSURANCE	0.0	636.5	636.5
SOCIAL SECURITY		(398.8)	(398.8)
DISABILITY INSURANCE		(66.5)	(66.5)
MEDICARE HOSPITAL INSURANCE		(132.0)	(132.0)
UNEMPLOYMENT INSURANCE		(30.4)	(30.4)
FEDERAL EMPLOYEES RETIREMENT CONTRIBUTIONS		(4.5)	(4.5)
RAILROAD RETIREMENT		(4.5)	(4.5)
EXCISE TAXES	23.3	46.6	69.9
ALCOHOL	(7.2)		(7.2)
TOBACCO	(7.7)		(7.7)
TELEPHONE AND TELETYPE SERVICES	(5.1)		(5.1)
HIGHWAYS		(33.1)	(33.1)
AIRPORTS AND AIRWAYS		(10.7)	(10.7)
HAZARDOUS SUBSTANCE SUPERFUND		(1.0)	(1.0)
OTHER	(3.3)	(1.8)	(5.1)
ESTATE AND GIFT TAXES	27.0	0.0	27.0
CUSTOMS DUTIES	18.3	0.1	18.4
MISCELLANEOUS	44.3	(2.1)	42.1
TOTAL	**1,200.7**	**682.3**	**1,883.0**

*THIS RECEIPT IS FROM THE HAZARDOUS SUBSTANCE SUPERFUND TAX.

SOURCE: THE OFFICE OF MANAGEMENT AND BUDGET

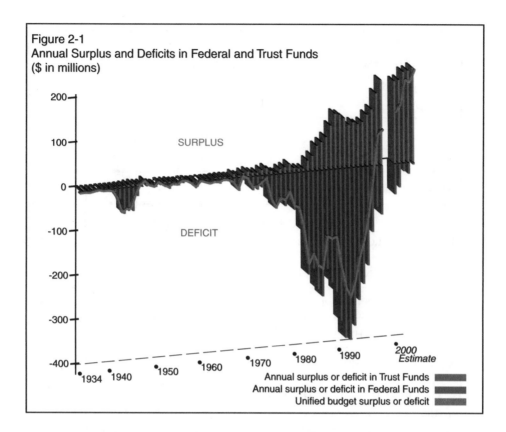

Figure 2-1
Annual Surplus and Deficits in Federal and Trust Funds
($ in millions)

This deficit in the Federal Funds is covered by borrowing money from the Trust Funds that now collect more money annually than they spend ($185 billion projected for FY 2000). Eventually, the Trust Funds will spend more than they collect as Social Security and Medicare spending exceed annual collections. At that time, the monies borrowed by the Federal Funds will have to be repaid.

After payments are made to the Trust Funds in FY 2000 for interest and the government share of trust fund program costs, only $916 billion will be available to cover Federal Fund outlays to the public of $984 billion. The difference of $68 billion (seven percent of the payments to the public from federal funds) will be financed by borrowing from the Trust Funds. (Table 2-3)

The Trust Fund surplus is higher than might be expected because some designated receipts are not being used. For example, The Nuclear Waste Disposal Fund collects about $0.6 billion each year but spends only $.2 billion. The budget assumes that the Airport and Airway Trust Fund each year will collect more money than will be spent on related programs (a surplus of $3 billion in 1999 with annual surpluses of more than $1.5 billion each year thereafter.)

TABLE 2-3
FEDERAL FUNDS AND TRUST FUNDS IN FY 2000
($ IN BILLIONS)

	FEDERAL FUNDS	TRUST FUNDS	TOTAL
RECEIPTS FROM THE PUBLIC	1,201	682	1883
PAYMENT OF INTEREST ON FUNDS BORROWED FROM TRUST FUNDS	(125)	125	0
OTHER PAYMENTS BETWEEN THE FUNDS*	(160)	160	0
AVAILABLE FOR EXPENDITURE	916	967	1,883
PAYMENTS TO THE PUBLIC	(984)	(782)	(1,766)
SURPLUS OR DEFICIT	(68)	185	117

* THIS INCLUDES THE FEDERAL GOVERNMENT'S SHARE OF SOCIAL INSURANCE PROGRAMS INCLUDING MEDICARE, UNEMPLOYMENT, AND CONTRIBUTIONS TO CIVILIAN AND MILITARY EMPLOYEE RETIREMENT PROGRAMS.

SOURCE: THE OFFICE OF MANAGEMENT AND BUDGET

Chapter 3

Receipts

Receipts in the federal budget reflect the collections that result from exercising the United States' sovereign, or governmental, powers.

Receipts consist of individual and corporate income taxes, social insurance taxes, excise taxes, compulsory user charges, customs duties, court fines, certain license fees, and other deposits.

In FY 2000, governmental receipts are estimated at $1,883 billion.

The Government also collects money through business-like or market-oriented activities.

These collections are called offsetting collections because they offset (reduce) the amount of new budget authority and outlays needed to cover fully the total costs of government programs. They are not combined with governmental receipts.

- For FY 2000, these collections (excluding monies collected from federal agencies) are estimated at $176 billion. (Table 3-1)
- These collections include fees for business-like activities such as the medicare supplemental insurance, postal service stamp sales, electric power sales, provision of health insurance benefits for government employees, admissions to national parks, national flood insurance premiums, and other user fees.
- The collections also include funds received from foreign sales of military equipment, spectrum auction sales, and rent from the Outer Continental Shelf.

Relationship Between Receipts and GDP

In 2000, governmental receipts are estimated at 20.7 percent of GDP. Only in 1944 during World War II, when Federal receipts reached 20.9 percent of GDP, has the Federal government consumed a larger portion of GDP.

TABLE 3-1
ESTIMATED FY 2000 RECEIPTS FROM THE PUBLIC
($ IN BILLIONS)

	FEDERAL FUNDS	TRUST FUNDS	TOTAL
GOVERNMENTAL RECEIPTS	**1,201**	**682**	**1,883**
INDIVIDUAL INCOME TAXES	900		900
CORPORATE INCOME TAXES	188	1	189
SOCIAL INSURANCE TAX AND CONTRIBUTIONS		636	636
EXCISE TAXES	23	47	70
OTHER	90	(2)	88
USER FEES AND OTHER OFFSETTING COLLECTIONS	**131**	**45**	**176**
USER FEES	**100**	**45**	**145**
POSTAL SERVICE	65		65
MEDICARE SUPPLEMENTARY INSURANCE		23	
FOREIGN MILITARY SALES FEES		13	
ELECTRIC POWER	9		
FEDERAL EMPLOYEE AND RETIREE HEALTH BENEFITS		5	
MILITARY HOUSING AND COMMISSARY FEES	7		
OTHER USER FEES	19	4	
OTHER OFFSETTING COLLECTIONS	**31**		**31**
SPECTRUM AUCTION SALES	5		5
OUTER CONTINENTAL SHELF RENT AND ROYALTIES	3		3
INTEREST, ROYALTIES, RENT, SALES OF PROPERTY AND PRODUCTS, CREDIT ACTIVITIES	14		14
OTHER	9		9
TOTAL GOVERNMENT REVENUE	**1,301**	**727**	**2,055**

Before the second World War, government receipts were less than 10 percent of GDP.

As defense spending increased during the war, government receipts increased, reaching almost 21 percent of GDP in 1944.

After the war, receipts as a percent of GDP dropped but remained higher than pre-war levels.

Since 1970, receipts have been relatively stable – varying between 17.2 and 19.7 percent of GDP, with an average of 18.4 percent. (Figure 3-1).

In the President's budget, receipts are estimated to decline to about 20 percent of GDP by 2004, and to remain at about that level thereafter.

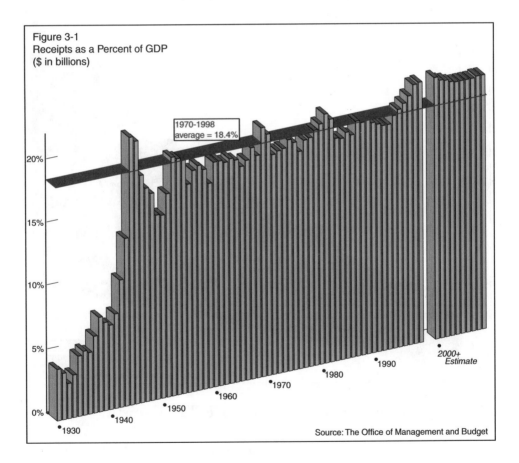

Figure 3-1
Receipts as a Percent of GDP
($ in billions)

1970-1998
average = 18.4%

20%

15%

10%

5%

0%

•1930   •1940   •1950   •1960   •1970   •1980   •1990   2000+
                                                              Estimate

Source: The Office of Management and Budget

Growth in Receipts

The estimated receipts in FY 2000 of $1,883 billion are $77 billion (4%) more than those in FY 1999 receipts.

From FY 1960 through FY 1998, government receipts increased at a compound annual rate of 3.2 percent. (GDP growth was 2.8 percent per year.)

In real terms, receipts are projected to grow about 2.6 percent between 1998 and 2000 and then a little over one percent per year after that. (Figure 3-2)

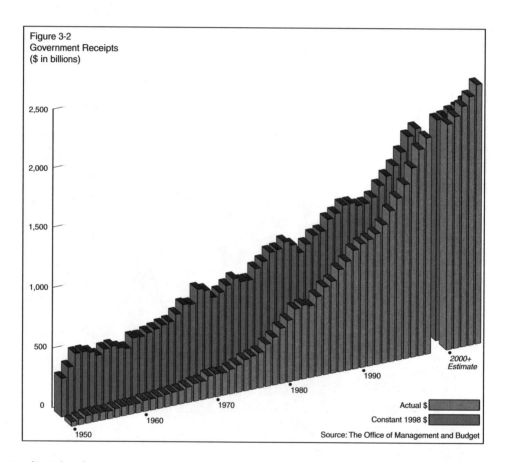

Figure 3-2
Government Receipts
($ in billions)

2000+
Estimate

1990

1980

1970

1960

1950

Actual $
Constant 1998 $

Source: The Office of Management and Budget

Individual Income & Social Insurance Tax Growth

In constant 1999$, almost all of the growth in receipts since 1950 has come from individual income tax and social insurance contributions and taxes. (Figure 3-3)

- Receipts from individual income taxes increased from about $130 billion in 1950 to more than $840 billion in 1998. They are projected to increase by 1.3 percent annually in real terms between 1998 and 2004.

- Social insurance contributions and taxes increased from $40 billion in the early 1950's to more than $580 billion in 1998. They are projected to increase by 2.2 percent annually in real terms between 1998 and 2004.

- Receipts from corporate income tax averaged almost $125 billion until 1993. They have grown significantly in recent years, reaching $192 billion in 1998. Between 1998 and 2004, these taxes are estimated to increase by 0.6 percent per year.

- The total receipts from other taxes remained relatively flat at about $100 billion from 1950 through 1993. Since then, they have increased significantly, reaching $135 billion in 1998. They are projected to increase by 3.7 percent per year between 1998 and 2004. The projected increase is due primarily to proposed tobacco and airport taxes, new fees, and increased revenues from highway taxes.

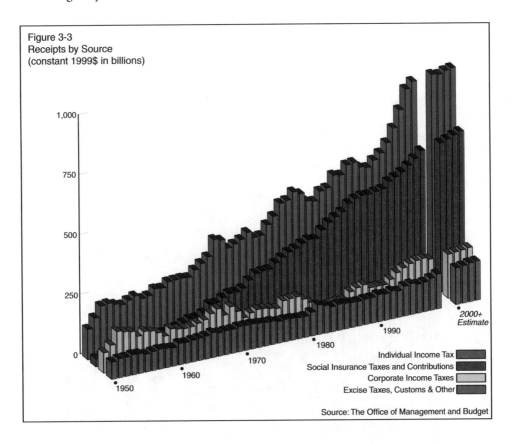

Figure 3-3
Receipts by Source
(constant 1999$ in billions)

Individual Income Tax
Social Insurance Taxes and Contributions
Corporate Income Taxes
Excise Taxes, Customs & Other

Source: The Office of Management and Budget

Shift From Social Insurance Contributions & Taxes

After years of growth, social insurance contributions and taxes have declined as a portion of receipts since 1992 due to increases in corporate and individual income taxes. (Figure 3-4)

- They provide funds for Social Security, Medicare, unemployment insurance, and government employee retirement programs.

- They now constitute about 34 percent of receipts, compared to about 10 percent in the early 1950's, 20 percent in the 1960's, 30 percent in the 1970's, 35 percent in the 1980's, and almost 37 percent in the early 1990's.

Individual income taxes now account for about 48 percent of receipts compared to 44 percent in 1992, and about 48 percent in the early 1980's. They are projected at about 47 percent after 2000.

Corporate income tax has declined to about 10 percent of receipts from more than 25 percent in the early 1950's, offsetting some of the increase in employer taxes for social insurance programs. This tax is projected to continue at about 10 percent of receipts in the future.

Other taxes declined from just under 20 percent in the 1950's to about eight percent of total receipts in 1998. They will remain at about that level.

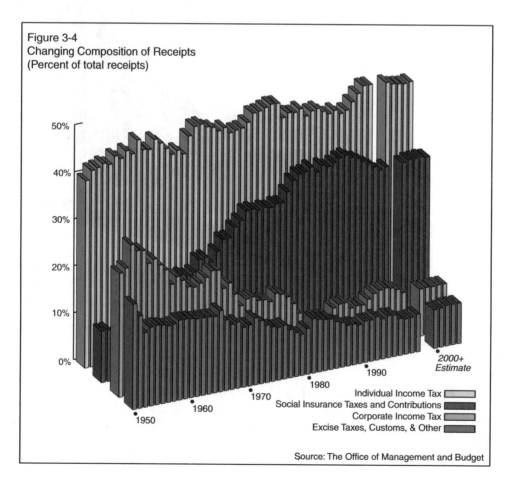

Figure 3-4
Changing Composition of Receipts
(Percent of total receipts)

Individual Income Tax
Social Insurance Taxes and Contributions
Corporate Income Tax
Excise Taxes, Customs, & Other

Source: The Office of Management and Budget

Receipts per Capita

On a basis of real dollars per capita, federal receipts have increased faster than GDP since 1992. This trend is expected to continue through FY 2000. (Figure 3-7) By 1998:

- Receipts were almost $6,500 per person;
- GDP per capita was almost $32,000; and
- After tax GDP per capita was over $25,000.

The Budget for FY 2000 implies this trend will be reversed in 2001 when GDP per capita will begin to grow faster than receipts per capita. Federal receipts per capita in real 1999$ will remain relatively flat at about $6,700 per year.

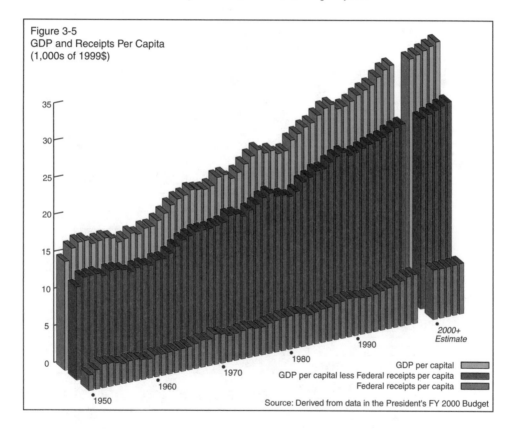

Figure 3-5
GDP and Receipts Per Capita
(1,000s of 1999$)

Tax Expenditures

Tax expenditures represent the government's forgoing some of the receipts it would otherwise receive. Examples of tax expenditures are deductions for mortgage interest from taxable income, and tax deferrals, credits, and exemptions. In FY 2000, tax expenditures are projected to cost the government about $617 billion in lost receipts. Some of the more significant tax expenditures are shown in Table 3-2.

25

Tax expenditures have the same effect on the budget as government spending; they just are not as visible.

- This system of priorities has developed over the years to further certain national objectives and to assist certain special interests.
- Eliminating tax expenditures would not increase tax revenue by $631 billion because of the effect they have on overall economic activity. For example, eliminating the mortgage interest deduction would affect the demand for housing, the market prices of existing homes, and the disposable income available for other things.
- Whole industries significant to the U.S. economy, such as home construction, banking, and life insurance depend on continuation of existing benefits provided through tax expenditures.

TABLE 3-2 TAX EXPENDITURES BY TYPE ESTIMATES FOR 2000 ($ IN BILLIONS)	
INCOME EXCLUDED FROM INCOME TAX	292
EMPLOYER PENSION PLAN	84
EMPLOYER CONTRIBUTIONS FOR MEDICAL INSURANCE PREMIUMS AND MEDICAL CARE	78
INTEREST	39
CAPITAL GAINS FORGIVEN AT DEATH	27
SOCIAL SECURITY BENEFITS FOR RETIRED WORKERS, DEPENDENTS AND SURVIVORS, AND DISABILITY INSURANCE	25
CAPITAL GAINS ON HOUSES	19
INDIVIDUAL RETIREMENT ACCOUNT (IRA), KEOGH CONTRIBUTIONS	15
WORKMEN'S COMPENSATION BENEFITS	5
INCOME TAXED AS CAPITAL GAINS RATHER THAN AS ORDINARY INCOME	41
INCOME TAXES DEFERRED TO LATER YEARS	48
ACCELERATED DEPRECIATION OF MACHINERY, EQUIPMENT, BUILDINGS AND HOUSING	42
INCOME FROM CONTROLLED FOREIGN CORPORATIONS	6
EXPENSES DEDUCTIBLE FROM INCOME	141
MORTGAGE INTEREST ON OWNER-OCCUPIED HOMES	55
NON-BUSINESS STATE AND LOCAL TAXES OTHER THAN ON OWNER-OCCUPIED HOMES	37
CHARITABLE CONTRIBUTIONS	26
STATE AND LOCAL PROPERTY TAX ON OWNER-OCCUPIED HOMES	19
MEDICAL EXPENSES	4
CREDITS AGAINST INCOME TAX	35
CHILD AND DEPENDENT CARE EXPENSES	21
EARNED INCOME CREDIT	5
PROJECT HOPE	5
CORPORATIONS RECEIVING INCOME FROM DOING BUSINESS IN U.S. POSSESSIONS	4
ALL OTHER ADJUSTMENTS THAT REDUCE TAXES	60
TOTAL	617
SOURCE: THE OFFICE OF MANAGEMENT AND BUDGET	

Chapter 4

Spending

Spending is projected at $1,766 billion in FY 2000, which is $39 billion (2.2 percent) more than in FY 1999.

From 1990 through 1998, federal spending grew at an real (after inflation) rate of 0.9 percent per year, compared to real annual increases of 3.5 percent from 1962 through 1990. The lower rate of spending growth was due in large measure to the budget procedures embodied in the Budget Enforcement Act of 1990, and subsequent extensions of these provisions, and to the cuts in defense spending made possible by the end of the Cold War. Almost all of the growth since 1990 has been in mandatory spending. (Figure 4-1)

The estimates in the President's FY 2000 budget indicate that most of the spending growth will continue to be in the mandatory category. These estimates, however, obfuscate what is really being proposed for the discretionary budget, that portion of spending covered in annual appropriations acts. Estimates for discretionary spending include offsets from the mandatory side of the budget beginning in 2000 and allowances contingent on Social Security reform beginning in 2001. Without these special adjustments, spending in the discretionary category would exceed the current legal limits by more than $17 billion in 2000, $39 billion in 2001, and $54 billion in 2002. This is described in more detail later in this chapter.

Growth in Mandatory Spending

In real terms, almost all of the spending growth has been in the mandatory category. Since the late 1960's real mandatory spending has increased by a factor of three. In contrast, real discretionary spending is at roughly the same level now as it was then.

In the early 1960's, mandatory spending was about one-third of all spending. By 1975, mandatory and discretionary spending were about equal. Now, mandatory spending is about two-thirds of the budget and it is projected to reach almost 69 percent by FY 2004. (Figure 4-2)

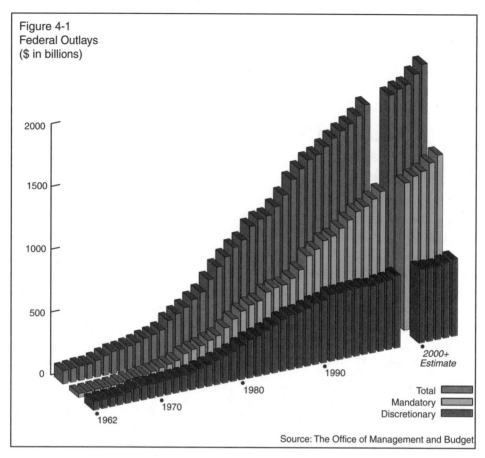

Figure 4-1
Federal Outlays
($ in billions)

Source: The Office of Management and Budget

Mandatory Spending

Mandatory spending is estimated at $1,174 billion in FY 2000, $28 billion (2.5%) more than in FY 1998. Three items account for more than 80 percent of mandatory spending – Social Security, health, and net interest.

- The major growth has occurred in health spending, which grew at more than 9 percent per year in constant dollars from 1967, when Medicare was started, through 1999. Health spending is projected to increase by $19 billion in FY 2000. From 2000 through 2004, health spending is expected to increase by 4 percent per year in real terms

- Net interest grew considerably during the mid-1980's due to the increase in the debt. In both actual and real dollars, net interest is projected to decline as a result of forecast budget surpluses.

- Social Security spending has been growing at about four percent per year in real terms since 1962. It is projected to grow at about two percent per year after FY 1999.

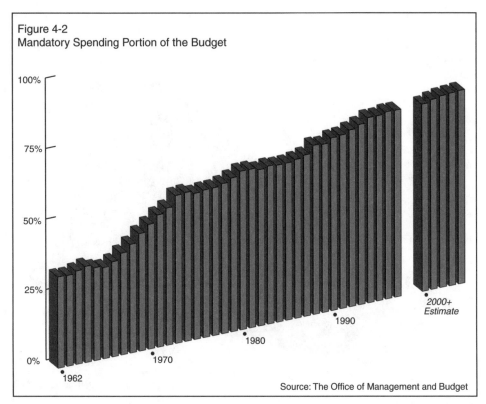

Figure 4-2
Mandatory Spending Portion of the Budget

100%

75%

50%

25%

0%

1962

1970

1980

1990

2000+
Estimate

Source: The Office of Management and Budget

- The "all other" category includes income security programs, offsetting receipts, deposit insurance, and a variety of relatively small activities. For FY 2000, an increase of $5 billion in projected. After FY 2000, real growth of about one percent per year is projected.

Discretionary Spending

Discretionary spending is projected at $592 billion in FY 2000, an increase of $10 billion (1.8 percent) over FY 1999.

Considerable change has taken place within the discretionary accounts over the last 30 years.

- National defense, which used to account for about 75 percent of discretionary spending, now accounts for 48 percent. From 1990 through 1999, real defense spending declined by more than three percent per year. A decrease of $2.7 billion is projected for FY 2000. Although spending in 2000 will be lower than in 1999, the budget authority requested for 2000 is $4.6 billion above the 1999 level. After FY 2000, real defense spending is projected to increase by 1.3 percent per year in real terms.
- International affairs spending has declined since it peaked in 1993. It now accounts for three percent of discretionary spending, down from four percent in 1990, and six percent in the mid-1960's. After FY 1999, international

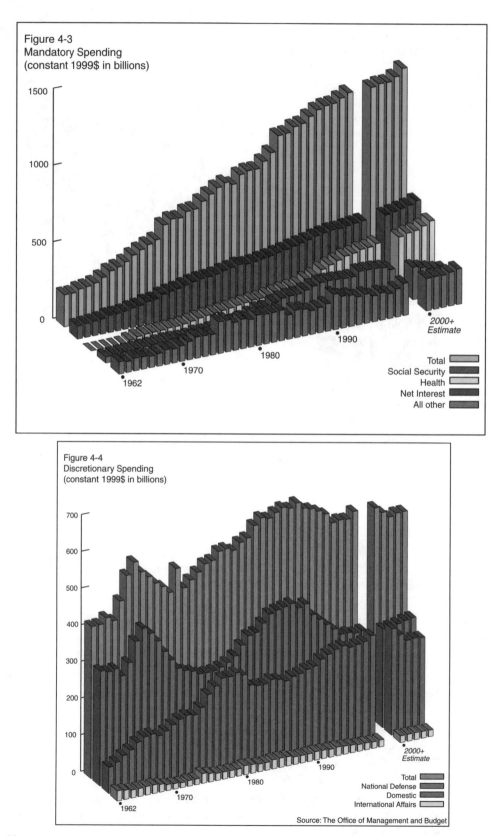

Figure 4-3
Mandatory Spending
(constant 1999$ in billions)

1500

1000

500

0

2000+
Estimate

1990

1980

1970

1962

Total
Social Security
Health
Net Interest
All other

Figure 4-4
Discretionary Spending
(constant 1999$ in billions)

700

600

500

400

300

200

100

0

2000+
Estimate

1990

1980

1970

1962

Total
National Defense
Domestic
International Affairs

Source: The Office of Management and Budget

30

spending is projected to increase slightly in actual dollars, but decline in real dollars at a rate of about one percent per year.

• Domestic spending has been increasing. From 1990 through 1999, domestic spending increased at a real rate of about 2.5 percent per year. An increase of $13 billion is proposed for FY 2000. After FY 2000, the President's budget projects a real decline of about 0.8 percent per year even with the assumption that additional funds will be made available after Social Security reform is enacted.

Working Around the Discretionary Caps

Limits on the level of discretionary funding for fiscal years 1998 through 2002 were established in the Budget Act of 1997. (A more detailed discussion of these is in Chapter 5.) A driving factor behind those limits was an overriding desire to achieve a balanced budget in 2002. That objective meant that programmatic factors were a second order consideration, especially in years after the immediate budget year. The difficult cuts in real spending levels were postponed until 2000, 2001, and 2002.

The FY 1998 budget was enacted consistent with the Budget Agreement without the need to resort to work-arounds.

For FY 1999, the problem became more difficult. In order to provide funding for all of the programs desired by the Administration and to stay within the legal spending limits, the President's Budget proposed to pay for additional discretionary spending through new user fees, a tobacco tax, a Superfund tax, and other mandatory offsets to the discretionary budget. Congress rejected the taxes, but did pass emergency appropriations of $20 billion at the end of the FY 1999 appropriations process. By law, these emergency appropriations were outside the spending limits in the Budget Act.

For FY 2000, the President's Budget again proposes discretionary spending above the legal limits. In an attempt to keep apparent spending as low as possible, the budget includes new user fees of almost $2 billion per year and a variety of budgetary devices such as incrementally funding the FY 2000 military construction program. Even with these adjustments, the budget proposal for FY 2000 exceeds the legal limits by $17.8 billion in budget authority and $17.1 billion in outlays. The differences are even greater in subsequent years.

To offset the excess spending, the Budget proposes new taxes, and other uses of mandatory revenue and savings in FY 2000. Because those are insufficient to offset fully the excess funding after FY 2000, the budget assumes, but does not propose, that additional funding will be made available after Social Security reforms are enacted. (Table 4-1)

TABLE 4-1
BRIDGE BETWEEN PRESIDENT'S FY 2000 BUDGET AND CURRENT SERVICE BASELINE
(DISCRETIONARY FUNDS; $ IN BILLIONS)

		2000	2001	2002	2003	2004	2000-04
PRESIDENT'S BUDGET							
	BA	555.0	590.9	594.8	607.4	619.9	2,968.0
	OUTLAYS	591.5	612.4	622.6	636.3	649.3	3,112.1
BASELINE: CAP IN 2000-02, CURRENT SERVICES AFTER THAT							
	BA	537.2	541.9	551.0	567.2	583.7	2,781.0
	OUTLAYS	574.4	573.3	568.2	584.1	599.9	2,899.8
DIFFERENCE: AMOUNT PRESIDENT'S BUDGET EXCEEDS GOALS							
	BA	17.8	49.0	43.8	40.2	36.2	187.0
	OUTLAYS	17.1	39.1	54.4	52.2	49.4	212.3
USE OF MANDATORY RECEIPTS AND SAVINGS TO OFFSET THE DIFFERENCE							
	BA	17.7	12.9	15.1	16.7	15.6	78.1
	OUTLAYS	17.7	12.9	13.5	15.8	15.3	75.2
TRANSFER OF CURRENT PAYGO BALANCES							
	BA/OUTLAYS	2.9	0.8	0.2	1.1		5.0
TOBACCO TAX							
	BA/ OUTLAYS	8.0	7.1	6.6	6.4	6.4	34.5
SUPERFUND TAX							
	BA/OUTLAYS	1.5	1.2	1.2	1.2	1.3	6.5
OFFSET FOR MILITARY RETIREMENT							
	BA/OUTLAYS	0.8	1.1	1.2	1.2	1.3	5.6
TOBACCO RECOUPMENT							
	BA			3.4	4.3	4.3	11.9
	OUTLAYS			1.8	3.3	4.0	9.1
REPLACE HARBOR SERVICES AND AIRPORT EXCISE TAX WITH HIGHER USER FEES							
	BA/OUTLAYS	1.6	1.6	1.5	1.4	1.3	7.5
HEALTH CARE AND STUDENT LOAN SAVINGS							
	BA/OUTLAYS	2.8	1.0	1.1	1.0	1.1	7.1
REMAINING SHORTFALL							
	BA	0.0	36.1	28.7	23.5	20.6	108.9
	OUTLAYS	0.6	26.2	40.9	36.4	34.1	137.0
DISCRETIONARY INCREASE RESULTING FROM SOCIAL SECURITY REFORM							
	BA		50.7	47.6	29.5	34.5	162.2
	OUTLAYS		26.3	40.9	36.5	34.1	137.7

Spending by Budget Function

All federal spending is categorized into 20 budget functions.

- This relates the spending to national objectives.
- A single department may have funding in several functions. The Department of Agriculture, for example, has discretionary funding in eight different budget functions.

A few budget functions account for most of the spending.

- Within the discretionary category, defense accounts for almost one-half of the outlays. The next major category is Education, Training, Employment and Social Services with eight percent.
- In the mandatory spending category, Social Security accounts for 35 percent, health and Medicare combined account for 28 percent, followed by net interest at 12 percent. (Table 4-1)
- National defense, Social Security, income security, health programs, and net interest account for almost 90 percent of all spending. (Table 4-2)

Tax expenditures show the budgetary impact of income tax deferrals, exemptions, and special benefits. The budget enumerates these tax expenditures and allocates them to the budget functions. (Tax expenditures are discussed in greater detail in chapter 3.)

- Tax expenditures are an indirect way to fund national objectives.
- Understanding completely the priorities of the federal budget requires examining the indirect tax expenditures in addition to direct federal outlays. (Table 4-3)
- Tax expenditures act as an incentive to direct private funds into housing, income security, training and education, and health.
- The outlay equivalent of the FY 2000 tax expenditures total $739 billion, which is equal to 42 percent of the level of direct outlays.

Annual Appropriations Acts

Funding for discretionary programs is provided in 13 annual appropriations acts. (Table 4-4)

- Each of the 13 appropriations acts is the responsibility of a separate subcommittee of the House and Senate Appropriations Committees.
- Assignments of programs to subcommittees tend to remain rather steady over time. Once a program is assigned to a subcommittee it tends to stay with that subcommittee regardless of organizational changes in the Executive Branch.

TABLE 4-2
FEDERAL SPENDING (OUTLAYS) BY BUDGET FUNCTION IN FY 2000
($ IN BILLIONS)

	DISCRETIONARY		MANDATORY		TOTAL	
	$	%	$	%	$	%
NATIONAL DEFENSE (050)	275	46%	-1	0%	274	16%
INTERNATIONAL AFFAIRS (150)	20	3%	-4	0%	16	1%
GENERAL SCIENCE, SPACE & TECHNOLOGY ((250)	19	3%	0	0%	19	1%
ENERGY (270)	3	1%	-5	0%	-2	0%
NATURAL RESOURCES & ENVIRONMENT (300)	24	4%	0	0%	24	1%
AGRICULTURE (350)	4	1%	11	1%	15	1%
COMMERCE & HOUSING CREDIT (370)	5	1%	1	0%	6	0%
TRANSPORTATION (400)	44	7%	2	0%	46	3%
COMMUNITY & REGIONAL DEVELOPMENT (450)	11	2%	-1	0%	10	1%
EDUCATION, TRAINING, EMPLOYMENT & SOCIAL SERVICES (500)	50	8%	13	1%	63	4%
HEALTH (550)	30	5%	123	10%	152	9%
MEDICARE (570)	3	0%	214	18%	217	12%
INCOME SECURITY (600)	42	7%	216	18%	258	15%
SOCIAL SECURITY (650)	3	1%	405	35%	409	23%
VETERANS BENEFITS & SERVICES (700)	19	3%	25	2%	44	2%
ADMINISTRATION OF JUSTICE (750)	27	5%	1	0%	28	2%
GENERAL GOVERNMENT (800)	13	2%	2	0%	15	1%
NET INTEREST (900)		0%	215	18%	215	12%
ALLOWANCES (920)	3	0%		0%	3	0%
UNDISTRIBUTED OFFSETTING RECEIPTS (950)	-3	0%	-43	-4%	-46	-3%
TOTAL	592	100%	1174	100%	1766	100%

SOURCE: THE OFFICE OF MANAGEMENT AND BUDGET

TABLE 4-3
TOTAL DIRECT (OUTLAYS) AND INDIRECT (TAX EXPENDITURES) SPENDING BY
BUDGET FUNCTION IN FY 2000
($ IN BILLIONS)

	OUTLAYS		TAX EXPENDITURES		TOTAL	
	$	%	$	%	$	%
NATIONAL DEFENSE (050)	274	16%	3	0%	277	11%
INTERNATIONAL AFFAIRS (150)	16	1%	15	2%	31	1%
GENERAL SCIENCE, SPACE & TECHNOLOGY ((250)	19	1%	2	0%	21	1%
ENERGY (270)	-2	0%	2	0%	0	0%
NATURAL RESOURCES & ENVIRONMENT (300)	24	1%	2	0%	26	1%
AGRICULTURE (350)	15	1%	1	0%	16	1%
COMMERCE & HOUSING CREDIT (370)	6	0%	267	36%	274	11%
TRANSPORTATION (400)	46	3%	2	0%	48	2%
COMMUNITY & REGIONAL DEVELOPMENT (450)	10	1%	2	0%	12	0%
EDUCATION, TRAINING, EMPLOYMENT & SOCIAL SERVICES (500)	63	4%	78	11%	141	6%
HEALTH (550)	152	9%	117	16%	269	11%
MEDICARE (570)	217	12%		0%	217	9%
INCOME SECURITY (600)	258	15%	149	20%	407	16%
SOCIAL SECURITY (650)	409	23%	25	3%	433	17%
VETERANS BENEFITS & SERVICES (700)	44	2%	3	0%	47	2%
ADMINISTRATION OF JUSTICE (750)	28	2%		0%	28	1%
GENERAL GOVERNMENT (800)	15	1%	70	9%	85	3%
NET INTEREST (900)	215	12%	1	0%	216	9%
ALLOWANCES (920)	3	0%		0%	3	0%
UNDISTRIBUTED OFFSETTING RECEIPTS (950)	-46	-3%		0%	-46	2%
TOTAL	1766	100%	739	100%	2504	100%

SOURCE: THE OFFICE OF MANAGEMENT AND BUDGET

TABLE 4-4
FY 2000 DISCRETIONARY BUDGET AUTHORITY BY APPROPRIATIONS BILL AND FUNCTION
(EXCLUDES ALLOWANCES, $ IN BILLIONS)

FUNCTION	SUBCOMMITTEE & BILL				
	AGRICULTURE, RURAL DEVELOPMENT & RELATED AGENCIES	COMMERCE, JUSTICE & STATE, THE JUDICIARY & RELATED AGENCIES	NATIONAL SECURITY	DISTRICT OF COLUMBIA	ENERGY & WATER DEVELOPMENT
NATIONAL DEFENSE		DOJ, DOT 0.4	DOD 262.9		DOE 12.4
INTERNATIONAL AFFAIRS	DOA 0.8	DOS, USIA 5.9			
GENERAL SCIENCE, SPACE & TECHNOLOGY					DOE 2.8
ENERGY					DOE 1.8
NATURAL RESOURCES & ENVIRONMENT	DOA 1.2	DOC, DOS 2.6			DOE. COE 4.5
AGRICULTURE	DOA 4.1				
COMMERCE & HOUSING CREDIT	DOA 0.6	DOC, SBA 4.8			
TRANSPORTATION		DOT 0.1			
COMMUNITY & REGIONAL DEVELOPMENT	DOA 0.8	DOC, SBA 0.5			
EDUCATION, TRAINING, EMPLOYMENT & SOCIAL SERVICES					
HEALTH	DOA, HHS 1.3				
MEDICARE					
INCOME SECURITY	DOA 4.6				
SOCIAL SECURITY					
VETERANS BENEFITS & SERVICES					
ADMINISTRATION OF JUSTICE		JUDICIARY, DOJ, OTHER 22.8			
GENERAL GOVERNMENT				DC 0.3	
TOTAL	13.4	37.1	262.9	0.3	21.5

TABLE 4-4 CONTINUED
FY 2000 DISCRETIONARY BUDGET AUTHORITY BY APPROPRIATIONS BILL AND FUNCTION
(EXCLUDES ALLOWANCES, $ IN BILLIONS)

FUNCTION	SUBCOMMITTEE & BILL				
	FOREIGN OPERATIONS	INTERIOR & RELATED AGENCIES	LABOR, HEALTH & HUMAN SERVICES, EDUCATION & RELATED AGENCIES	LELGISLATIVE BRANCH	MILITARY CONSTRUCTION
NATIONAL DEFENSE					DOD 5.4
INTERNATIONAL AFFAIRS	DOS, FOREIGN ASSIST. EXIM BANK 14.6				
GENERAL SCIENCE, SPACE & TECHNOLOGY					
ENERGY		DOE 1.0			
NATURAL RESOURCES & ENVIRONMENT		DOI, DOA 8.2			
AGRICULTURE					
COMMERCE & HOUSING CREDIT					
TRANSPORTATION					
COMMUNITY & REGIONAL DEVELOPMENT		DOI 1.2			
EDUCATION, TRAINING, EMPLOYMENT & SOCIAL SERVICES		DOI, ED, OTHER 2.0	DOI, ED, HHS 49.0	CONGRESS 0.3	
HEALTH		HHS 2.4	HHS, DOL 26.9		
MEDICARE			HHS 2.9		
INCOME SECURITY			DOL, HHS, SSA 7.1		
SOCIAL SECURITY			SSA 3.2		
VETERANS BENEFITS & SERVICES			OTHER 0.1		
ADMINISTRATION OF JUSTICE			HHS, ED 0.2		
GENERAL GOVERNMENT		DOI 0.2		CONGRESS 2.3	
TOTAL	14.6	15.0	89.4	2.6	5.4

TABLE 4-4 CONTINUED
FY 2000 DISCRETIONARY BUDGET AUTHORITY BY APPROPRIATIONS BILL AND FUNCTION
(EXCLUDES ALLOWANCES, $ IN BILLIONS)

FUNCTION	SUBCOMMITTEE & BILL			
	TRANSPORTATION & RELATED AGENCIES	TREASURY, POSTAL SERVICE, & GENERAL GOVERNMENT	VETERANS AFFAIRS, HUD, & INDEPENDENT AGENCIES	TOTAL
NATIONAL DEFENSE	DOT 0.3		NSF 0.2	261.6
INTERNATIONAL AFFAIRS				21.3
GENERAL SCIENCE, SPACE & TECHNOLOGY			NASA, NSF 16.4	19.2
ENERGY				2.8
NATURAL RESOURCES & ENVIRONMENT	DOT 0.1		EPA 7.2	23.8
AGRICULTURE				4.1
COMMERCE & HOUSING CREDIT		POSTAL SERVICE 0.2	HUD -0.2	5.4
TRANSPORTATION	DOT 12.4		NASA 1.0	13.5
COMMUNITY & REGIONAL DEVELOPMENT			HUD, FEMA TREAS 6.4	8.9
EDUCATION, TRAINING, EMPLOYMENT & SOCIAL SERVICES			NCS 0.8	52.1
HEALTH				30.6
MEDICARE				2.9
INCOME SECURITY			HUD 18.5	30.2
SOCIAL SECURITY				3.2
VETERANS BENEFITS & SERVICES			DVA 19.2	19.3
ADMINISTRATION OF JUSTICE		TREAS. 3.3	HUD 0.1	26.4
GENERAL GOVERNMENT		TREAS, GSA, OPM, EOP, ARCHIVES 9.9		12.7
TOTAL	12.8	13.4	69.6	558.0

ABBREVIATIONS USED IN TABLE 4-4	
COE	CORPS OF ENGINEERS
DC	DISTRICT OF COLUMBIA
DOA	DEPARTMENT OF AGRICULTURE
DOC	DEPARTMENT OF COMMERCE
DOD	DEPARTMENT OF DEFENSE
DOE	DEPARTMENT OF ENERGY
ED	DEPARTMENT OF EDUCATION
DOI	DEPARTMENT OF THE INTERIOR
DOJ	DEPARTMENT OF JUSTICE
DOL	DEPARTMENT OF LABOR
DOS	DEPARTMENT OF STATE
DOT	DEPARTMENT OF TRANSPORTATION
EOP	EXECUTIVE OFFICE OF THE PRESIDENT
EPA	ENVIRONMENTAL PROTECTION AGENCY
FEMA	FEDERAL EMERGENCY MANAGEMENT AGENCY
GSA	GENERAL SERVICES ADMINISTRATION
HHS	HEALTH AND HUMAN SERVICES
HUD	DEPARTMENT OF HOUSING AND URBAN DEVELOPMENT
NASA	NATIONAL AERONAUTICS AND SPACE ADMINISTRATION
NCS	NATIONAL AND COMMUNITY SERVICE
NSF	NATIONAL SCIENCE FOUNDATION
OPM	OFFICE OF PERSONNEL MANAGEMENT
SBA	SMALL BUSINESS ADMINISTRATION
SSA	SOCIAL SECURITY ADMINISTRATION
TREAS	DEPARTMENT OF THE TREASURY
TVA	TENNESSEE VALLEY AUTHORITY
USIA	UNITED STATES INFORMATION AGENCY

- Thus, a single department may deal with several subcommittees. For example, the Department of Health and Human Services receives funds from the Labor, Health and Human Services, Education and Related Agencies, the Appropriations Act for Agriculture, Rural Development and Related Agencies Appropriations Act, and the Interior and Related Agencies Appropriations Act.

- Several subcommittees may deal with a single function. Programs for International Affairs, for example, are divided among three subcommittees. Funds for international programs are included in the Foreign Operations Appropriations Act, the Agriculture, Rural Development and Related Agencies appropriations act and the bill Commerce, Justice and State, the Judiciary and Related Agencies appropriations act.

- A single subcommittee may provide funding for programs in several functions. For example, the Commerce, Justice and State, Judiciary, and Related Agencies appropriations act programs fall in eight different budget functions.

Chapter 5

Overview of the Budget Process

At any one time, the Federal government is working on three budgets:

- Execution of the budget for the current fiscal year that began on October 1;
- Congressional action on the budget for the fiscal year that will begin next October 1; and
- formulation of the President's budget that will be sent to the Congress next February.

For example, during calendar year 1999, the agencies are executing the FY 1999 budget, Congress is reviewing the President's request for FY 2000, and the Executive Branch is formulating the President's Budget for FY 2001. (Figure 5-1.)

While the processes for making budget decisions may seem to be unwieldy and excessively complex, they are, in fact, rather simple and straightforward. They seem complex because the issues are difficult, the processes consume a lot of time, and many people have a stake in the outcome.

Steps in the Process

A summary of the process follows. Subsequent chapters provide further details. Dates for key steps are set in law, though there are no legal penalties for delays.

- Formulation of the President's budget. This budget reflects the president's priorities on spending and revenue for the budget year and the four following fiscal years. The process starts about 12 months before the president must submit a budget to Congress (the first Monday in February of each year). The Budget describes the President's priorities and includes details on each of more than 1,300 appropriation accounts.
- Congressional action. This begins with receipt of the President's budget and ends with enacted appropriations. The Congress can accept, modify, or completely disregard the President's request. Although it often does not happen, all action on the budget should be finished before the fiscal year starts on October 1. Products produced include the following:

41

Figure 5-1
Formulation of the President's Budget

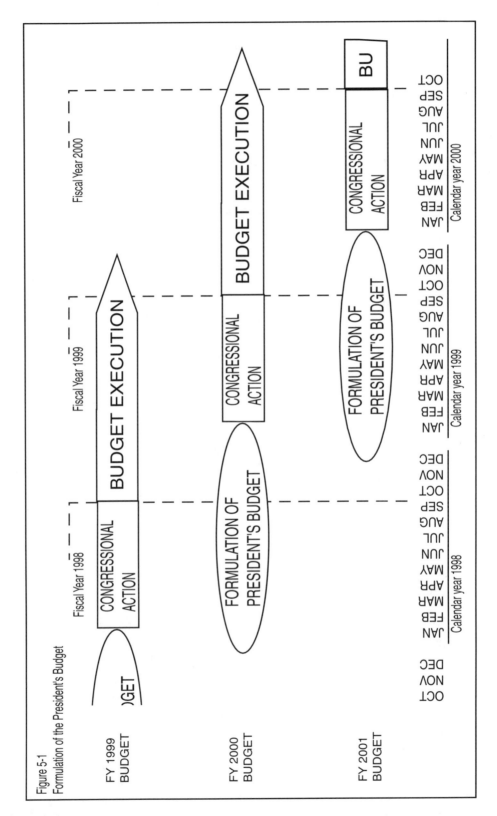

- Concurrent Budget Resolution. This master plan for Congressional action is due by April 15. It is an agreement between the House of Representatives and the Senate specifying spending for the entire government by individual budget function, e.g., national defense, energy, housing, etc., and the expected revenue for the budget year and the four following fiscal years. The resolution does not require Presidential approval.
- Reconciliation bills. These bills change existing revenue and direct spending laws to make them consistent with the spending and revenue provisions in the Budget Resolution. The reconciliation bill does not address the spending included in the annual appropriations bills described below. Normally, one omnibus reconciliation bill includes all of the spending changes required by the Resolution. This is to happen by June 15.
- Authorization bills. An authorization bill provides the legal basis for a program and establishes program requirements. Some programs have permanent authorization; others require new authorization each year. Generally, the Congress authorizes a program before providing appropriations.
- Appropriations bills/acts. Annual appropriations acts provide funding for the 33 percent of the budget that requires annual funding (Figure 1-1). Mandatory spending does not require annual appropriations. There are 13 annual appropriations acts. Funding cannot exceed the limits set in the Budget Resolution without a waiver passed by the Congress. The House is supposed to complete action on all annual appropriation bills by June 30.

Each house performs each step independently. Differences are resolved in conferences of key House and Senate members. After both houses agree to the conference bill, the result is termed an enrolled bill and is sent to the president for approval. The president can approve the measure or veto it and send it back to the Congress for reconsideration.

- Program Execution. This phase begins at the start of the fiscal year and ends when the appropriations are spent or expire, which can take several years. Subject to certain limitations, some departments can transfer appropriated funds between programs and all Departments may reprogram funds within programs, permitting them to respond to changes in program performance and requirements. The president can request supplemental funds if necessary. The president also can propose that appropriated funds be rescinded or deferred.

Legislation to Help Control the Deficit

There have been two main legislated attempts to control the deficit. These laws placed limits on how much can be appropriated, and created a process called sequestration to remove budget authority when the legislated limits are breached.

The first major effort was the Balanced Budget and Emergency Deficit Control Act of 1985, commonly known as Gramm-Rudman-Hollings (GRH), which established the process of sequestration.

- Sequestration is the automatic elimination of budget authority.
- In GRH, sequestration was to occur if deficit limits established in the GRH law were exceeded.

The second major attempt to legislate deficit reduction was the Budget Enforcement Act (BEA) of 1990, which established several new rules, set limits on annual appropriations, and revised the sequestration process for fiscal years 1991 through 1995. These rules were extended through FY 2002 by the Budget Enforcement Acts of 1993 and 1997.

- The BEA established a Pay-As-You-Go (PAYGO) rule for mandatory spending and receipts.
    - The cumulative effects of enacted legislation affecting mandatory spending or receipts must not increase the deficit.
    - Following the end of a session of Congress, an estimate is made of the net effect on the deficit of enacted laws affecting mandatory spending and receipts.
    - Any net increase in the estimated deficit for the current year and the budget year combined is to be removed by sequester of mandatory spending programs. The purpose of the PAYGO sequester is to uniformly reduce spending across-the-board. Less than three percent of all mandatory spending is sequestrable, however, because some programs are exempt and there are limits on the amounts that can be sequestered for certain other programs.
- Each of the BEA's placed limits (caps) on discretionary appropriations and estimated outlays.
    - The caps apply to both the President's budget and Congressional appropriations.
    - For fiscal year 1998, discretionary funding was divided into three categories – Defense, Non-Defense, and Violent Crime Reduction – and caps were placed on each category. For 1999, the yearly outlay caps were added for highways and mass transit. For 2000, Defense and Non-defense are combined into a single category. The caps as of February 1999 are shown in Table 5-1.

TABLE 5-1
DISCRETIONARY SPENDING LIMITS REPORTED IN THE PRESIDENT'S BUDGET
($ IN BILLIONS)

	1998	1999	2000	2001	2002
NON-DEFENSE					
BUDGET AUTHORITY	256.1	289.7			
OUTLAYS	286.3	276.2			
DEFENSE					
BUDGET AUTHORITY	271.8	279.9			
OUTLAYS	269.1	272.6			
VIOLENT CRIME REDUCTION					
BUDGET AUTHORITY	5.5	5.8	4.5		
OUTLAYS	4.8	5.0	5.6		
HIGHWAYS					
BUDGET AUTHORITY					
OUTLAYS		22.0	24.6	26.2	26.7
MASS TRANSIT					
BUDGET AUTHORITY					
OUTLAYS		4.4	4.1	4.9	5.4
OTHER					
BUDGET AUTHORITY			532.7	541.9	551.0
OUTLAYS			540.1	542.2	536.1
TOTAL					
BUDGET AUTHORITY	533.4	575.4	537.2	541.9	551.0
OUTLAYS	560.2	580.2	574.4	573.3	568.2

- Emergency supplemental appropriations are outside the caps. An emergency is whatever the president and the Congress decide it is.
- If the BA provided in appropriations acts for a fiscal year exceeds the BA cap, or the outlays estimated to result from this BA exceed the outlay cap, the BA is reduced through sequestration. Spending for most discretionary programs is reduced by a uniform percentage though some programs are exempt and special rules apply to other programs.
- Scorekeeping rules have been adopted for tracking the budgetary effect of Congressional action.
    - The CBO, under guidance from the Budget Committees, provides an estimate of the cost of every bill being considered by the Congress. These scorekeeping estimates provide the basis for potential points of order on the floor of the House or Senate. A point of order is a formal objection to a measure that violates a budget rule.
    - The OMB provides estimates of the cost of each bill. These estimates are the basis for determining whether or not a sequester may be necessary.
    - Reports accompanying the Budget Enforcement Acts provide guidance for scorekeeping. They describe specific rules that will be used for determining the cost of credit programs, operating and long-term leases, asset sales, and other matters.
    - Because scorekeeping will always require some judgment, there can be significant differences between Congress and the Administration over how certain items should be scored. Resolution of some scorekeeping issues can even require consultation between the President and Congressional leadership.

Operation of the Sequestration Process

Sequester procedures under the BEA include the following steps:

- "Preview" reports are published by OMB and CBO when the President submits the budget.
    - They discuss the status of discretionary and PAYGO sequestration based on current law.
    - They explain the adjustments required by law to the discretionary caps.
- "Update" reports are published in August. An OMB report is due August 20th providing the effects of Congressional action taken since the "preview" report.
- A "final" report by OMB is published at the end of a session of Congress.
    - OMB's final report to the President and Congress 15 days after the

end of a session determines whether a sequester is needed.

- The report triggers a sequester if appropriations enacted during the current year exceed the caps or if the cumulative effect of PAYGO legislation would increase the deficit.
- OMB estimates are the basis for the sequester orders issued by the President. The President's order may not change the OMB report.
- CBO prepares a report using its scorekeeping rules. The Director of OMB must explain any differences between the OMB and CBO estimates.
- The General Accounting Office prepares a compliance report.

- From the end of a session of Congress through the following June 30th, discretionary sequesters take place whenever an appropriations act for the current fiscal year causes a cap to be exceeded.
  - This ensures that supplemental appropriations enacted during the fiscal year are covered by the budget enforcement provisions.
  - Because a sequester in the last quarter of a fiscal year might be too disruptive, a sequester that otherwise would be required then is to be accomplished by reducing the limit for the next fiscal year

By law, the receipts and outlays of Social Security (the Federal Old-Age and Survivors Insurance and the Federal Disability Insurance trust funds) and the Postal Service Fund are excluded from the budget totals and from the calculation of the deficit for Budget Enforcement Act purposes.

Congressional Procedures

Over time the Congress has developed rules that help maintain discipline during the budget process.

- Certain actions that could affect the budget or achievement of the budget resolution are prohibited and are subject to being ruled out of order.
- In the House, a waiver to the prohibition is handled by a "special rule" reported by the Rules Committee. All House special rules require a simple majority for passage.
- The Senate has tougher rules in that some prohibitions require 3/5 vote of the Senate to override.
- Examples of major types of legislation and resolution amendments that are prohibited and the processes necessary to override the prohibitions are listed below.

Prohibitions that require 3/5 vote of Senate to override:

- Consideration of an annual appropriations bills before the Appropriations Committee has made its spending subdivisions;

- Legislation that would cause total spending to exceed or revenues to fall below the aggregate spending or revenue levels for the Budget year or for the total of the five years covered by the resolution;
- Legislation that exceeds a spending allocation or subdivision made under the budget resolution for the first Budget year or for the total of all fiscal years for which spending allocations or subdivisions are made;
- Amendment to a reconciliation bill that is not deficit neutral;
- Reconciliation legislation that recommends changes in Social Security;
- Budget resolution that provides for discretionary spending limits to be exceeded;
- Direct spending or revenue legislation that increases the deficit during the period of the most recently adopted resolution and the following five years; and
- Non-germane amendments to resolution or reconciliation legislation (Byrd Rule).

House and Senate prohibitions that require a simple majority in both houses to override:

- Legislation providing new contract, borrowing, or credit authority that exceeds the amounts in appropriations acts,
- Spending, revenue, or debt-limit legislation for a fiscal year before a budget resolution for that year (or in the Senate, a resolution covering that year) has been adopted.

Possible Changes to the Budget Process

Reforms of the budget process may produce savings. Examples include the following:

- Congress could review mandatory spending programs annually. As stated earlier, the annual appropriation process currently considers only one-third of all Federal spending.
- Congress could place a limit or cap on mandatory spending like the one on discretionary spending. The challenge would be on how to distribute the funds among the mandatory programs, especially those programs funded by trust funds that are in a surplus position.
- Certain Congressional procedures could be tightened. For example, rules could be adopted that would prohibit including programs in conference bills that were not included in either the House or Senate bills. Another change would be to reduce the cap on discretionary spending applicable to a house of Congress whenever that house reduces spending for a program during floor debate on an appropriations bill.

The priority for spending reductions has greatly diminished as a result of the large budget surpluses projected from current law.

Chapter 6

Formulation of the President's Budget

"He [the President] shall from time to time give to the Congress Information of the State of the Union, and recommend to their Consideration such Measures as he shall judge necessary and expedient;"
Constitution, Article II, Section 3

By law, the President must submit a budget to the Congress by the first Monday in February each year.

- The budget reflects the President's priorities.
- The budget includes a detailed plan for revenues and spending in the fiscal year that will start eight months later on October 1 (the "budget year").
- The budget provides actual data on the most recently completed fiscal year, updated information on the current fiscal year, and planning estimates for four fiscal years following the budget year.
- It may propose changes to previously appropriated budget authority (BA).

The process for formulating the President's request receives less public exposure than the Congressional process. Except for occasional White House announcements about areas targeted for budget increases, and leaks from agencies, program managers, contractors, and communities concerned about departmental and White House budget decisions, there is relatively little detailed or substantive coverage in the mass media.

All departments and agencies and the Executive Office of the President are involved in the process.

- OMB manages the process for the President.
- The National Economic Council (NEC) created by President Clinton provides a forum for cabinet officials and top White House officials to discuss program and policy priorities.

- The Council of Economic Advisers, OMB, and the Treasury Department jointly develop economic assumptions for the budget. These assumptions cover inflation, real growth in the economy, interest, and unemployment.

Shortly after sending the budget for one fiscal year to Congress, work begins on the next fiscal year's budget as shown in Figure 5-1 in the preceding chapter.

Initial planning begins with the estimates for the outyears (years beyond the budget year) included in the previous budget. OMB, in consultation with the NEC, uses these figures in developing budget targets to be provided to the departments and agencies in the spring. (Figure 6-1)

Throughout the spring and summer, the departments and the Executive Office of the President conduct policy studies and program evaluations that can change the distribution of funds among departments and programs. For example, decisions flowing from a review directed by the Executive Office of the President on launch vehicles for space flight could affect funding proposals for the National Aeronautics and Space Administration and the Department of Defense (DOD).

Departmental reviews can also change the proposed allocation of funds among departmental programs. Most departments have extensive internal review processes. The DOD has the most intensive process with a policy review and detailed program review each year. DOD planning includes preparation of a detailed six-year plan that addresses the funding for every line item in the defense budget. Most other departments concentrate on only the budget year.

In July, OMB issues guidance on budget concepts and rules that the departments must follow in preparing their budget proposals.

In early September, the departments submit detailed proposals to OMB.

- The proposals generally reflect the OMB guidance and the results of the spring and summer policy studies, Congressional action on the last request, and actual program performance. The proposals are to include information required by the Government Performance and Results Act (GPRA) on outcomes and output anticipated at the proposed budget levels. GPRA is discussed in detail in Chapter 7.
- Departmental requests often exceed the planning estimates issued by OMB and in total the amount the President can request under current law.

During September and October, OMB staff review the requests.

- OMB Examiners hold hearings with departmental representatives to review the consistency of the request with Presidential policy and federal responsibilities, program performance, and the validity of the pricing and scheduling assumptions.

Figure 6-1
Formulation of President's Budget

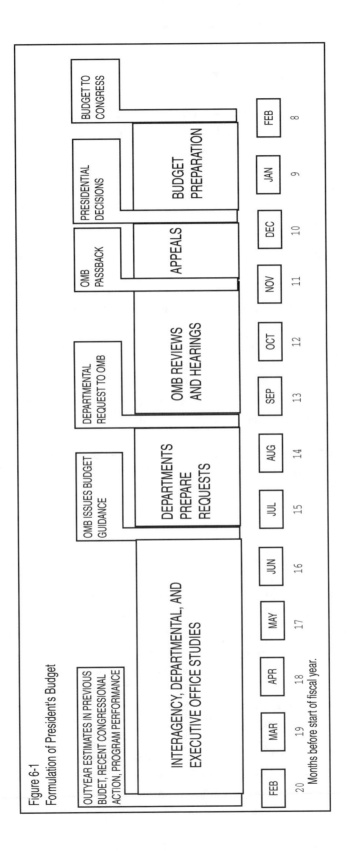

FEB	MAR	APR	MAY	JUN	JUL	AUG	SEP	OCT	NOV	DEC	JAN	FEB
20	19	18	17	16	15	14	13	12	11	10	9	8

Months before start of fiscal year.

OUTYEAR ESTIMATES IN PREVIOUS BUDET, RECENT CONGRESSIONAL ACTION, PROGRAM PERFORMANCE

INTERAGENCY, DEPARTMENTAL, AND EXECUTIVE OFFICE STUDIES

OMB ISSUES BUDGET GUIDANCE

DEPARTMENTS PREPARE REQUESTS

DEPARTMENTAL REQUEST TO OMB

OMB REVIEWS AND HEARINGS

OMB PASSBACK

APPEALS

PRESIDENTIAL DECISIONS

BUDGET PREPARATION

BUDGET TO CONGRESS

- OMB and departmental policy officials discuss Presidential and departmental priorities.

In late October and early November, the OMB Director reviews the requests.

- OMB staff present issue papers that analyze the department's request, provide options to the request, and comment on likely Congressional and public reaction. Budget tables show the possible distribution of funds among departments and budget functions.
- Policy officials in OMB, the NEC, and other parts of the Executive Office of the President provide views on program priorities and trade-offs among departments and functions.

Just before Thanksgiving, the Director "passes back" decisions to the Departments on what is to be included in the budget.

The departments generally appeal OMB passback decisions.

- They often appeal specific program adjustments and the overall budget level for the department.
- OMB and the department will attempt to reach agreement.
- If the department and OMB cannot reach agreement on a major issue, the issue is sent to the President for resolution.

Before the end of December, the President will make final decisions on the open issues.

During January, OMB and the departments reconcile the numbers and print the budget documents.

In February, the President submits the budget to Congress.

- The documentation includes a budget message from the President, a description of the President's priority programs, and supporting information.
- The Budget Appendix, a book comparable in size to the telephone book of a large metropolitan area, includes every spending account in the budget. Currently there are more than 1,300 spending accounts in the budget.
- The departments provide detailed justification data to the relevant Congressional Committees for each program. This information is cleared by OMB before it is sent to the Congress.

On July 15 each year, OMB submits to Congress an update of the budget estimates, the "Mid-Session Review." This document shows the effect of laws enacted since the budget submission, changes to economic assumptions, and budget changes proposed by the President.

Special Procedures for the Department of Defense

There are special procedures for the joint review of military department proposals by OMB and the Office of the Secretary of Defense (OSD).

The Secretary of Defense does not submit a budget to OMB in September. Instead, the military departments in September submit their requests to both OMB and OSD.

As part of the joint review process, OMB participates in all phases of DOD's planning, programming, and budgeting system, though the degree of participation varies among administrations.

OMB's role in DOD's three-phased process is as follows:

- Planning phase at start of calendar year:
    - OMB reviews planning guidance for consistency with existing policy and approved funding levels, alerts the OMB Director and other White House staff to proposed policy changes and the potential impact on department funding.
- Programming phase in spring and early summer:
    - OMB staff participate on issue teams that evaluate service proposals, making sure that issues of interest to the White House are addressed and that all proposed alternatives are consistent with budget and policy rules.
- Budgeting phase in the fall:
    - Defense Comptroller and OMB staff hold joint hearings with the military departments and work jointly on DOD Program Budget Decisions; OMB coordinates issues with other White House staff.

Usually, there is at least one meeting with the President, the Vice President, the Secretary of Defense, the OMB Director, and the Security Advisor on the defense budget.

- The level of the defense budget generally is the major issue:
    - With caps on discretionary spending, each dollar spent on defense is a dollar not available for other purposes and each dollar spent for defense is one that could be used to offset tax cuts or to reduce the deficit;
    - The potential effects of higher and lower budget levels are discussed.
- High-priority programs such as military force readiness including personnel pay and benefits are also discussed.

Chapter 7
Government Performance and Results Act

The Government Performance and Results Act of 1993, commonly referred to as "GPRA" or "the Results Act," is a new tool designed to improve governmental decision-making and to make government managers accountable for results.

The Results Act has been integrated into the budget process and it should affect the allocation of funds among programs. It will have little effect on the level of overall Federal spending, which is determined through the budget resolution process.

GPRA formalizes the steps that successful managers in government, the private sector, and non-profit organizations take, either formally or informally, in managing their organizations. It has three essential components:

- A strategic plan, which defines an agency's missions and goals;
- An annual performance plan, which defines in measurable terms the planned level of performance during the year to achieve those missions and goals; and
- An annual performance report, which compares the actual results to the planned results for the year.

Whether the Act will have a lasting effect on government programs and budgets depends on how Congress uses the information in the strategic and performance plans. If the Congress uses the information in making annual appropriations, the Results Act will make a difference. If there is no clear effect on appropriations, the act will die a slow death and add to, rather than reduce, the cost of government operations.

Background

Presidents and the Congress have long searched for ways to improve government decision-making and management.

Recent Presidents have initiated various measure designed to improve decision-making and management of the Executive Branch. These included:

- Planning, Programming, and Budgeting System (PPBS) initiated in the Department of Defense in the early 1960's and expanded to all Departments by President Johnson. PPBS was an attempt to improve decision-making by allocating resources to output categories, evaluating alternative ways of achieving the desired outputs, and taking a five-year look at resource requirements.
- Management by Objectives (MBO) initiated in the Nixon Administration in the early 1970's and restarted by the Bush Administration in the late 1980's. MBO was a process for defining and reporting progress on key administration objectives.
- Zero-Base Budgeting (ZBB) initiated in 1977 by President Carter. This process was designed to prioritize projects within Departments and on a government-wide basis in order to make sure the programs and activities with the greatest benefits were funded.

All of these initiatives had the purpose of improving decision-making in the Executive Branch by setting funding priorities through the systematic evaluation of missions, programs, and alternatives. Except for the continued use of PPBS in the Department of Defense, none of these management tools survived beyond the end of the Administration initiating them. Most were overly complex and focused on the Executive Branch with little or no involvement of Congress and no attempt to obtain bipartisan support. Further, the processes were top down and not integrated throughout the departmental budget systems.

The "Results Act" differs from the previous attempts in three key ways. It is a joint venture of Congress and the Executive Branch, it is law, and it requires consultation with Congress and others who will be affected by or have an interest in a Department's plans.

The Act applies to all Executive Branch Departments and Agencies, Government Corporations, and independent establishments except the Central Intelligence Agency (CIA), the Panama Canal Commission, the Postal Rate Commission, and the General Accounting Office. Although exempted by the Act, the CIA is implementing the Results Act voluntarily. Special provisions apply to the Postal Service.

Relationship of Results Act to the Budget Process

GPRA has been integrated into OMB Circular A-11, which is the document that establishes the procedures, forms and other guidance for the preparation of the President's Budget. Part 2 of the guidance is dedicated to GPRA. This makes the strategic plan the underpinning of the budget. The performance plans and reports provide the details on annual performance and actual results.

The timing of budget activities and GPRA actions is shown in Figure 7-1. The new activities related to GPRA are shown below the timeline arrow. Each of the GPRA activities is discussed later in this chapter.

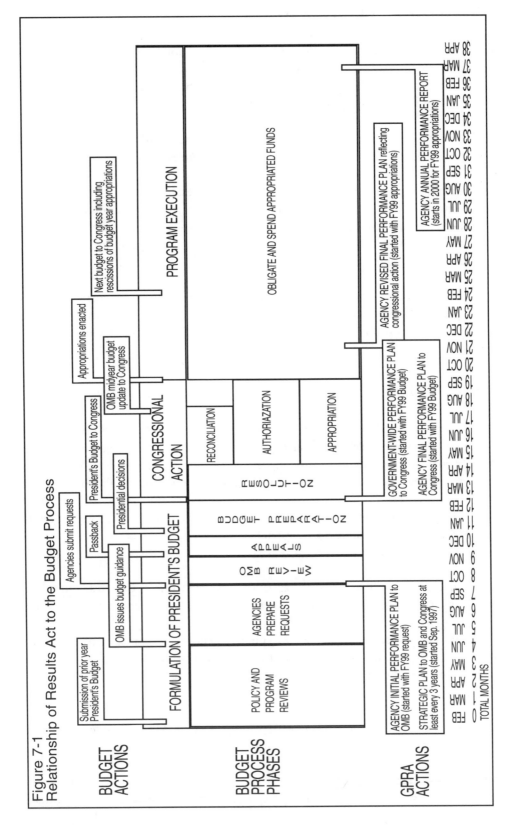

Figure 7-1
Relationship of Results Act to the Budget Process

Managerial Flexibility Waivers

Federal managers as a general rule are limited in their ability to shift resources within programs and to exercise other forms of managerial discretion common throughout the private sector. Rather than being held accountable for results, Federal managers are generally held accountable for following procedures.

GPRA provides some authority for waiving non-statutory administrative procedures pertaining to the internal allocation and use of resources.

Performance plans may include proposals to waive certain administrative procedures and controls. These include limits on personnel staffing and compensation, and restrictions on funding transfers among the budget categories for contractual services (object classification 20) and personnel compensation (11), personnel benefits (12), equipment (31) , and land and structures (32) of each annual budget.

A waiver proposal must describe the anticipated effects on performance and quantify the expected improvement in performance. This requirement places a significant burden of proof on the agencies to justify the benefits of proposed waivers.

Strategic Plans

The centerpiece of GPRA is the strategic plan, which covers the next five fiscal years. This plan states the mission of an organization, lays out the long-term goals and strategy for carrying out that mission, and indicates the needed level of resources. The resource levels are to be consistent with those projected in the President's budget.

The first formal Strategic plans covering fiscal years 1998 through 2002 were submitted to OMB and to the Congress in September 1997. The plans are to be revised and resubmitted every three years.

Before submitting the final plans, the agencies consulted with the Congress and solicited the views and suggestions of entities potentially affected by or interested in the plan.

OMB has encouraged the agencies to submit agency-wide plans. An agency with disparate functions, however, is permitted to prepare strategic plans for each of its major components or programs and to provide an agency-wide overview linking the plans.

The next set of plans by law are due in September 2000. OMB has requested the plans by March, 2000.

For each major function and operation of an agency the strategic plan is to provide a comprehensive mission statement and general goals and objectives. The OMB guidance states that support-type activities and operations can be omitted. OMB guidance recommends that the mission statement be "...brief, defining the basic purpose of the agency, with particular focus on its core programs and activities. In addition, the mission statement may include a concise discussion of enabling or authorizing legislation, as well as identification of issues that Congress specifically charged the agency to address."

The general goals and objectives are to include a description of:

- the operational processes, skills and technology, and the human, capital, information, and other resources (including regulations and tax expenditures) required to achieve the goals;
- the relationship between the general goals and objectives and the annual performance goals;
- factors beyond the agency's control that could significantly affect achievement of the goals and objectives; and
- the program evaluations used in setting the goals and objectives and a schedule for future program evaluations.

The goals and objectives must be clear and permit a future assessment as to whether they were or are being achieved. As pointed out in OMB guidance, brevity and conciseness will likely characterize plans that are useful and widely read.

OMB guidance requests the agencies to summarize in their transmittal letters to OMB and the Congress any views received from entities outside the Executive Branch that disagree, in a substantive and germane way, with the courses-of-action presented in the plan. The letter also is to contain a description of any significant contribution to the preparation of strategic plans made by non-Federal entities.

Congressional Review of Strategic Plans

Agencies provided draft strategic plans to the Congress in the summer of 1997. Some agencies placed their draft plans on the Internet and invited public comments.

This first attempt demonstrated how difficult it is to prepare precise, comprehensive, and terse statements of missions and goals for Departments that have many different programs.

Each agency took the path that it thought most appropriate:
- The Department of Defense used for its strategic plan the recently completed Quadrennial Defense Review (QDR). The QDR examined likely defense mission requirements over the next several years and identified the goals and objectives to implement those missions.
- Some agencies discussed the missions they are assigned in law.
- Some agencies addressed the missions they would like to perform.

Because GPRA is a high priority, "good government" effort, the Congress sought outside advice and help on how to implement the new process. Groups of specialists in various areas such as energy and science have provided comments on draft plans. The Council for Excellence in Government sponsored reviews of the plans and advised Congress, OMB, and the agencies on ways to make the plans as useful as possible.

The Congress reviewed the plans with assistance from the General Accounting Office (GAO), which devised a system for grading the plans.

- Out of a maximum score of 105, the average plan was graded at 29.9.
- The low grades reflected a variety of deficiencies including weaknesses in defining strategies for achieving general goals and objectives and in relating general goals to annual performance goals, lack of adequate data systems for measuring progress, and inadequate attention to program evaluations and other management problems.

Many of the plans reportedly failed to address statutorily-required elements. Majority Leader Armey expressed strong concern about this in his letter of August 7, 1997,

"...it is inexcusable for agencies to submit for Congressional consultations draft plans that do not even purport to address statutory elements."

Although almost all of the departments and agencies submitted final strategic plans in September 1997 that were judged to be better than the draft plans, the plans were still considered to be inadequate. Among the more pointed comments were those included in a November 1997 report "Towards a Smaller, Smarter, Common Sense Government, the RESULTS ACT: It's the Law." This report issued by House majority Leader Armey, the Chairmen of the House Committees on Budget, Appropriations and Government Reform and Oversight, and Senator Craig, Chairman of the Senate Republican Policy Committee, included the following:

"Agencies have a long way to go in developing fully acceptable strategic plans. The poor state of the strategic plans makes it even more important that agencies and OMB produce high quality performance plans..."

"The premise of the Results Act was that strategic plans would lay a good foundation for the annual performance plans to follow. Unfortunately, this has not yet happened. We hope that next year's performance plans can at least partially compensate for the deficiencies in the strategic plans and get Results Act implementation back on track."

"We expect agencies to submit another round of strategic plans by September 30 of next year that reflect substantive input from the Congress as well as substantial quality enhancements."

"Congress should view the submission of inadequate plans by agencies as an invitation to clarify that agency's mission and goals through reauthorizations, funding and legislative efforts..."

Annual Performance Plans

The Annual Performance Plans provide linkage between the general goals in the strategic plan and agency operations.

For each general goal in the strategic plan, the annual performance plan should include one or more performance goals that address program quality and quantity. These target levels of performance need to be defined with precision and expressed in objective, quantifiable, and measurable form.

Performance goals may be stated as "outcomes" or "outputs."

- "Outcomes" are the final results of government programs. To measure outcomes, there must be a clear definition of the expected result at the beginning of the program, e.g., deterrence of attack on the United States, completion of the census, development of a flu vaccine, etc. Outcome goals should be included in annual plans when their achievement is scheduled for the fiscal year covered by the plan. Outcomes in many cases are difficult to state for annual, continuing programs.
- "Outputs" are the result of government activity. They are items considered to be important toward achievement of an outcome. An output measure views the level of program activity or effort in a quantitative manner e.g., number of pilots to be trained per year or qualitative manner, e.g., level of customer satisfaction. The most useful output measures are those used by agency officials in day-to-day operations.
- Over-reliance on output measures, to the neglect of outcomes, is likely to be a general weakness of most performance plans.

Performance indicators measure or assess the achievement of the stated outputs and outcomes.

- The indicator is a value (number) or characteristic.
- Several indicators may be needed to measure quantity, quality, timeliness, cost, and outcomes.
  - Examples of quantitative indicators are production and number of transactions.

- Examples of qualitative indicators are timeliness, error rates, maintenance or repair intervals, complaints, and customer satisfaction levels.
- Particularly useful are indicators that relate the level of program activity to unit cost measures such as cost per unit of service, or cost per unit of output.
- GPRA calls for two types of performance plans – agency plans and a government-wide plan.

Agency Performance Plans

These are to include the performance goals for the agency's programs, the indicators that will be used to measure performance, a description of how the measured values will be verified, a summary of the needed resources, and an identification of any proposed waivers of administrative requirements. The plans also must describe the processes, skills and technology, and the human, capital, information, or other resources required to meet the goals.

- Each agency is to submit to OMB on September 30 each year an "initial" performance plan that is consistent with its budget proposal. The plan is to cover all components of the agency. OMB will use this information in developing budget issues for resolution by the Director and the President. Issue papers prepared by OMB staff will show the effect of alternative funding levels on proposed performance indicators.
- When the President's Budget is completed, the agencies, with OMB consultation, will prepare a "final" performance plan that is consistent with the President's Budget proposals. After publication of the government-wide performance plan discussed below, each agency will submit copies of its final plan to the relevant Congressional authorization and appropriation subcommittees, and make the plan available to the public.
- Congressional appropriation actions could alter the proposed performance levels in the annual performance plan. Any significant effects are to be addressed by the agency in its annual performance report (discussed later), or by issuing a revised annual performance plan.
- If a "Revised Final" plan is issued, it should be completed prior to the start of the fiscal year, and provided to OMB, the appropriate congressional committees, and made available to the public.

Federal Government Performance Plan

- A Federal Government Performance Plan is to be submitted with the annual budget of the United States Government for each year.

- In preparing the plan, OMB will use the more significant goals in the agency performance plans. Waivers of requirements and controls must be included.
- The government-wide plan does not have to be revised to reflect Congressional action.

Performance goals are to be expressed in a quantifiable and measurable form for a program activity at the proposed budget level.

OMB Circular A-11 encourages agencies, "... to consider changes to the budget account structure that enable agencies to present both budget and performance information in a more thematic or functional way, thereby facilitating the understanding of programs and measures of performance."

The first set of performance goals were submitted with the FY 1999 budget. As was the case with the first set of strategic plans, the goals were a good first step, but improvements were needed. It was not evident that this first set of performance goals had any significant effect on the actions of the Congress in appropriating funds to programs.

Annual Performance Reports

Each agency must prepare an annual performance report that compares the actual performance during the previous fiscal year to the goals in the plan, and describes the corrective action being taken in the current fiscal year, if necessary, to get the program back on track. If the agency's annual performance plan was revised after final Congressional action, the performance report should compare the actual performance to (1) the goals in the revised plan and (2) the goals in the government-wide plan submitted by OMB with the budget.

The first performance reports are to be submitted on March 31, 2000, covering activities in FY 1999. After that, annual reports are due each year on March 31.

Each report will:

- review the progress toward achieving the target goals during the year;
- evaluate the performance plan for the current fiscal year based on the actual performance in the completed year;
- explain the corrective actions recommended for missed goals;
- describe the use and effectiveness of any waivers; and
- summarize the findings of program evaluations completed during the year.

Performance reports are to be submitted to the appropriate authorization, appropriations, and other committees of the Congress and made available to the public upon request.

For many programs, especially those involving investments, the impact of the program may not occur until after the performance report is submitted.

Performance Budgeting

The line-item budgets sent to the Congress show much money the President proposes to spend on each program, and how that money should be allocated among various accounts. It shows how the money will be spent, but often does not show what is to be accomplished.

A budget showing a direct relationship between proposed spending and expected results, along with the anticipated effects of higher or lower amounts would be more useful. With that information, the Congress can decide on a appropriate level of output to fund in the appropriations bill.

GPRA requires a two-year pilot project in performance budgeting in at least five Federal programs, beginning in FY 1998, with a report to Congress from OMB on the results by March 31, 2001.

Pilot Projects

The Act requires that key features be tested on a pilot project basis.

- Performance Measurement. This was tested extensively for three years (FY1994-96). The results are described below. The pilot performance projects provided real experience for OMB to use in developing guidance for full-scale implementation and for the Departments in implementing GPRA.
- Managerial Flexibility. This was to be tested during fiscal years 1995-96. At least five of the pilot performance project agencies were to test "managerial accountability and flexibility" to see if flexibility increased the chances for project success. Several pilot projects were nominated, but none were approved. After passage of GPRA, changes to various laws and regulations eliminated the problems that GPRA flexibility was to test. Further, the agencies found it difficult to relate the flexibility to changes in measurable goals and objectives.
- Performance Budgeting. Under the law, this is to be tested in fiscal years 1998-99, including an alternative budget display for the selected pilot projects in the fiscal year 1999 budget. OMB proposed to delay the test one year and to present the new budget display in the fiscal year 2000 budget. This extra time is considered necessary to permit the agencies to improve their cost accounting systems.

The schedule in the Act for pilot projects is shown in the following table.

TABLE 7-1 SCHEDULE FOR GPRA PROJECTS	
OCTOBER 1, 1993	**ANNUAL PERFORMANCE PLANS AND REPORTS:** 10 PILOT PROJECTS SELECTED FOR FYs 1994, 95, 96
OCTOBER 1, 1994	**MANAGERIAL FLEXIBILITY WAIVERS:** 5 PILOT PROJECTS SELECTED FOR FYs 1995 AND 96
MAY 1, 1997	OMB REPORTS ON PILOT PROJECTS
JUNE 1, 1997	GAO REPORTS ON PILOT PROJECTS
SEPTEMBER 30, 1997	**PERFORMANCE BUDGETING:** 5 PILOT PROJECTS SELECTED FOR FYs 1998 AND 99
JANUARY 1998	**PERFORMANCE BUDGETING:** FY 1999 BUDGET TO INCLUDE PERFORMANCE BUDGET FORMAT FOR PILOT PROJECTS
MARCH 31, 2001	OMB REPORT ON PERFORMACE BUDGETING PILOT PROJECTS

Performance Measurement

GPRA specified that at least ten agencies, reflecting a representative range of Government functions and capabilities, be involved in pilot projects testing performance measurement.

Participation exceeded the minimums required by law. Due to agency interest in understanding performance measurement and in obtaining experience in a broad array of program types, there were three rounds of project nominations. In the first round, a total of 53 pilot projects in 21 departments and agencies were designated as pilot projects during fiscal years 1994-96. In the second and third rounds, additional projects were included as pilot projects in fiscal years 1995-96. In total, all 14 cabinet departments and 14 independent agencies participated with a total of over 70 individual pilot projects.

Findings from the May 19, 1997, OMB report on the results of the pilots are summarized below:

• Without the pilot projects there would be little prospect for successful implementation of GPRA government-wide. Over the three years there was improvement in the agency's abilities to set goals, and to measure and report performance against these goals. Based on this experience, it is expected that the first several years of government-wide implementation, "...will be lumpy as well." At the beginning of implementation, "...it would be unrealistic to expect that there will be a uniformly high level of quality of agency plans and reports across the government."

- As agencies gained experience during the pilot projects, they "... were able to identify key measures for determining program success and accomplishment and this helped in producing concise, brief, and informative plans."
- The pilot projects demonstrated the necessity of a strategic plan. Those agencies that started without a strategic plan had difficulty defining performance goals.
- Some goals were not measurable and the plans generally did not describe ways to determine whether the goal was achieved.
- Some agencies used the means or processes for achieving a goal in lieu of the goal. This reflected the fact that in some cases, the processes are under the control of agency managers, but the actions of others could have a significant effect on program outcomes. Based on this experience, measuring the output of Federally funded programs administered by States or local governments will be a challenging task.
- Costs for preparing performance plans and reports were low. No pilot program needed additional funding to prepare the required performance plans and reports.
- The pilot program, "...affirmed that virtually every activity done by government can be measured in some manner." The measurements may be difficult or even imperfect, but innovative managers will find ways to measure performance.

Actual experience with the first set of strategic plans and performance plans confirmed the relevance of the OMB findings.

Opportunities and Pitfalls

Preparation of clear, precise, and terse plans is not easy. The development of such plans, however, provides a vehicle for government departments to communicate their goals and objectives to the public. Consequently, the Results Act provides an opportunity for significant improvement in government operations.

- GPRA should lead government agencies to take greater interest in the development of long-range goals and plans. Most departments and agencies do little serious planning beyond the budget year. Currently, only the Department of Defense has a comprehensive five year plan. Good, long-range plans should identify future resource requirements and permit more informed decisions now.
- Serious long-range plans reviewed and accepted by key congressional committees could lead to more stability in agency planning. This does not mean that programs will necessarily be stable. Rather it means that Congress and the Executive may be able to agree on long range plans and goals and stick to those plans.

- If implemented carefully, the new management tools may result in additional funding or more stable funding for programs that perform well and reduced funds for programs that are ineffective or inefficient.
- Politics will continue to play an important role in the budget. There have been rules on benefit-cost analyses for decades, but they have not kept projects with benefits less than their costs from being funded. If political forces are evident, even projects with poor results may be funded notwithstanding the requirements of GPRA. GPRA will, however, shed additional light on low performers and provide measurements of performance that up to now have been unavailable. The combination of tight budgets and demonstrated low performance may be sufficient to affect the funding of ineffective programs.

On the other hand, there are significant obstacles and challenges that will have to be overcome for this new process to be useful in the long run.

- Government agencies must take seriously the development of strategic plans, performance goals and measurements under GPRA. Agency heads must be involved and use the results for agency management. If this does not occur, GPRA will become just another reporting requirement taking resources away from more productive use.
- Development of useful, reliable quantitative measures is essential. Considerable effort and care will be needed to develop measures that are not one-dimensional or result in misplaced priorities. Valid measures must consider output or outcomes, customer satisfaction, and quality.
- Quantitative measures must reflect reasonable estimates of achievable aims. In an attempt to appear to be responsive, some agencies may attempt to promise more than can be delivered at projected resource levels. For example, some agencies are currently projecting increases in output and efficiency with declining real resource levels. Although this is highly desirable and what the taxpayers expect, this may prove impossible to achieve. In that event, the public will have cause to doubt the sincerity of government planning, which will create credibility problems. As always, the best approach is honesty.
- The Congress will need to make some budget decisions based on GPRA products. This will not be easy because even weak programs have political constituencies. The Congress and the Administration already have a good sense about the programs that work well and those that do not. Whether additional information will change the political decision-making process remains to be seen. Time will show whether politics can be separated from program funding.
- There is a risk that the Administration and Congress may not agree on strategic plans and performance measures for some agencies. Congressional committees reviewing the plans may have different priorities than the departments and the Administration. For example, bipartisan agreement does not currently exist concerning what each department of government should be doing, or even whether all of the agencies should exist. Whether such differences can

be resolved sufficiently to make GPRA work is an open issue.

- Agency managers must see GPRA as an important and useful management tool. Promotions, bonuses, and other rewards must go to managers who meet their objectives. If rewards are not linked to successful implementation of GPRA requirements there will be little incentive for managers to take GPRA seriously. Because it is formulated as a management strategy, GPRA implementation is not something that can be left solely to agency budget officials.

Chapter 8
Congressional Processes

"No Money shall be drawn from the Treasury, but in Consequence of Appropriations made by Law..."
Constitution, Article 1, Section 9, paragraph 7.

"All Bills for raising Revenue shall originate in the House of Representatives; but the Senate may propose or concur with Amendments as on other Bills."
Constitution, Article 1, Section 7, paragraph 1.

The Congressional process has four main elements:

- Development of a Concurrent Budget Resolution (CBR);
- reconciliation of permanent law to the requirements of the CBR;
- authorization of new and annual programs; and
- appropriation of funds for annual programs.

In contrast to the rather closed process for formulating the President's budget, the Congressional process is open except for some committee hearings on national security issues and bill mark-up sessions.

Citizens and organizations interested in particular legislation can insert themselves into the process:

- They can meet with their elected Representatives and Senators,
- they can request time to appear in hearings before the committees; and
- they can recommend actions and propose language for inclusion in bills.

The President, White House staff, and rest of the Executive Branch follow each step closely.

- The end result of all parts of the process are bills that the President must approve or veto.
- The Administration informs the Congress of its views on each bill through a Statement of Administration Position (SAP). The SAP states whether the Administration supports the bill, recommends changes to the bill as written, or whether the President's advisors would recommend a veto.

The departments devote considerable time and effort to the committees.

- They ensure that the members of the authorization and appropriations committees understand the department's priorities and problems.
- Policy officials and staff testify before the committees that have roles in the congressional budget process. All written testimony provided to the Congress is first cleared by the OMB to ensure that it is consistent with the President's budget.

The committees work more closely with the departments than with the White House.

- They tend to be protective of their client agencies.
- Issues on which the departments did not prevail during development of the President's budget often resurface in Congress.

Committee staff members play key roles in Congressional action.

- Departmental budgets often contain so many line items that it is impossible for a Representative or Senator to understand all the details. Committee staff master the details.
- Committee staff write committee reports to accompany appropriations bills, and which explain the committee's actions and provide further direction to the departments. Although such directions in "report language" are not legally binding, the departments do not want to irritate the committees by ignoring them.

The Congressional Budget Office (CBO) supports the Congressional budget process.

- CBO prepares periodic reports, special analyses, a book of possible budget reductions and budget baseline estimates for Congressional action.
- CBO publishes a review of the President's budget shortly after it is submitted to Congress that includes a repricing of the budget using CBO, rather than OMB, economic assumptions.
- Congressional committees use CBO-developed outlay rates to evaluate the effect of alternative budget proposals.

- CBO provides the Congress estimates of the budget impact of each bill.

Congress has many opportunities to address a specific program. For each bill (authorization and appropriations), the opportunities are as follows:

- during House and Senate Subcommittee mark-up of a bill;
- during full committee mark-up in the House and Senate of a bill;
- during floor action in each house on the bill; and
- during Conference committee action on the bill. (These committees can take actions not included in either house's bill.)

An important step in the House that is not applicable to the Senate is the rule for floor debate. Before a bill is taken to the House floor, a rule is created by the Rules Committee and passed by the House. The rule states the time for debate, the amendments that will be considered, and the order of the amendments.

Figure 8-1 (Congressional Budget Process) shows the steps in the Congressional process and the approximate timing.

Concurrent Budget Resolution

The first step in the Congressional process is the preparation of a Concurrent Budget Resolution (CBR). The CBR lists the budget priorities of the Congress for the next five fiscal years. It will, for example, state whether the Congress wants to reduce or increase taxes, or increase or reduce defense or domestic spending, or adjust entitlement programs.

The CBR is not a law and does not require Presidential approval. Nevertheless, the Congress generally attempts to obtain Presidential agreement because the laws implementing the CBR will be sent to the President for approval. Due to potential differences between the Congress and the President, the Congress did not adopt a budget resolution in FY 1999.

The CBR includes budget aggregates, functional allocations of spending, and reconciliation instructions.

- Aggregates include total revenues, total new budget authority, total outlays, the surplus or deficit, the debt limit, and total new direct loan obligations and new primary loan guarantee commitments.
- Functional allocations show total spending, both mandatory and discretionary, by budget function.
- Reconciliation directives instruct the committees regarding the dollar amount of revenue or spending changes they must achieve by revising permanent laws concerning revenue and spending.

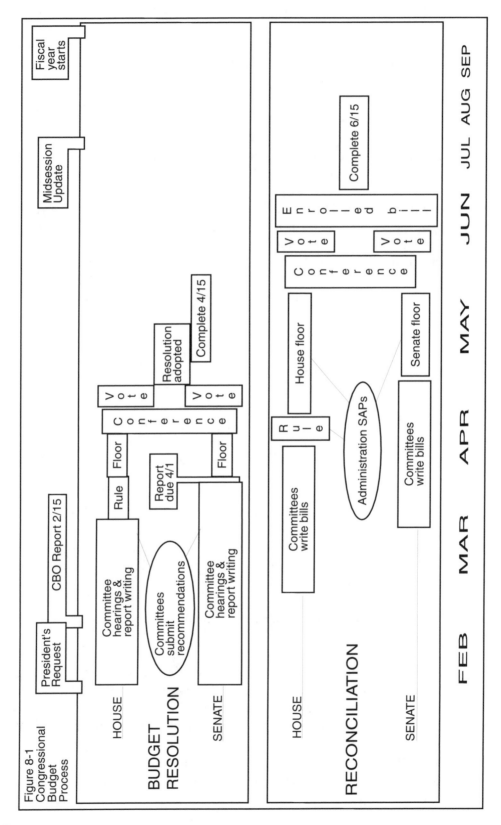

Figure 8-1
Congressional
Budget
Process

BUDGET RESOLUTION

RECONCILIATION

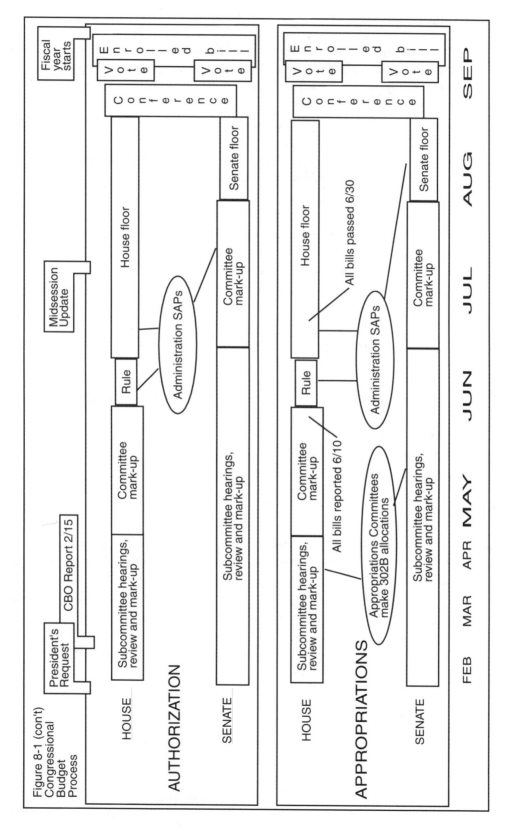

Figure 8-1 (con't)
Congressional
Budget
Process

AUTHORIZATION

APPROPRIATIONS

FEB   MAR   APR   MAY   JUN   JUL   AUG   SEP

Major steps in developing the CBR include the following:

- In mid-March, six weeks after the President submits a budget proposal, each Congressional committee provides funding and revenue recommendations for the programs under its jurisdiction to the Budget Committee of the relevant house.
- The House and Senate Budget Committees develop resolutions for their respective houses.
- Budget Committee reports specify the programmatic assumptions used in developing the amounts for each budget.
- The Senate Budget Committee is to report to the Senate by April 1.
- Each house passes a resolution.
- A House/Senate Conference resolves differences between the two resolutions and develops a consensus position.
- Each house votes for or against the Conference position.
- Current law requires the Congress to adopt a resolution by April 15 though the date is seldom met.

After the resolution is adopted, the total budget authority and outlays specified in it are allocated among House and Senate committees with jurisdiction.

- Discretionary spending is under the jurisdiction of the Appropriations Committees.
- Amounts proposed by the committees may not exceed the amounts in the resolution.

Reconciliation

Reconciliation directives in the resolution require Congressional authorizing and Finance committees to achieve certain revenue or spending targets through changes in permanent laws.

- The instructions specify the dollar amount of change that each committee must achieve.
- Which laws to change and how to change them is left to the committees.

Reconciliation action can include the following:

- increasing or reducing tax levels;
- changing the benefits or eligibility requirements for entitlement programs; or
- requiring government agencies to charge fees.

Congress often enacts a single Omnibus Budget Reconciliation Act (OBRA) that includes all the legislation necessary to carry out all of the reconciliation directives in the resolution.

Action on reconciliation is to be completed by June 15. Like other Congressional deadlines on budget matters, however, the reconciliation date is seldom met.

- Reconciliation issues address tax and entitlement programs, which are quite controversial and involve considerable give-and-take with the President.
- For fiscal years 1996 and 1997, the Congress never finished reconciliation due to differences with the President over Medicare and other politically sensitive programs.

Program Authorization

The Congress usually enacts legislation that authorizes appropriations for a particular program. This is how the committees with jurisdiction over the laws pertaining to a department or government function control the spending in their area of responsibility.

The authorization of an appropriation typically precedes the enactment of the appropriation itself. This does not always happen, however, because Congress may enact an appropriation that contains its own "authorization."

An authorization may originate in either house.

In addition to providing authority for an appropriation, an authorization may also include:

- limits on the amount that can be appropriated for a program;
- the types of costs that can be incurred; and
- other direction affecting program management and program content.

Some programs require annual authorization, other programs receive authorization for a specified number of years, and still others are authorized indefinitely.

- The military programs of the Department of Defense (DOD) are an example of programs that require annual authorization. Each year the Congress authorizes all DOD programs, addressing every line item in the appropriations bill.
- Funding for regulatory agencies, by contrast, is usually authorized for a specified number of years.
- Examples of authorizing legislation for an indefinite number of years and therefore outside the annual appropriations process include Social Security, retirement benefits for Federal government employees, and Medicare.

Appropriations

The Appropriations Committee in each house allocates the discretionary amounts approved in the CBR among its subcommittees. These allocations, referred to as 302b allocations (in reference to 302b of the Congressional Budget Act), provide linkage between the CBR and the funds in the 13 annual appropriations bills. Although the Budget Resolution includes "appropriate" levels of discretionary spending by budget function, the Appropriations Committee is not required to follow that guidance. The operative direction in the Resolution is only the total funding allocated to the Committee.

As previously stated, Congress usually authorizes a program before it appropriates funds. In the absence of an authorization, however, inclusion of funds for a program in an appropriations bill generally provides Congressional approval, unless there is a law specifically prohibiting the expenditure.

A separate subcommittee is responsible for each of the 13 annual appropriations bills.

- The subcommittees and their areas of jurisdiction are shown in Table 4-3 in Chapter 4.
- Having a subcommittee deal with several budget functions can lead to strange trade-offs among the funding for programs and departments. For example, funds requested by the President for certain international activities can be allocated to domestic programs during the appropriations process.

The appropriations bills must be consistent with 302b allocations.

- The committees, however, have some latitude in deciding what to include in each bill.
- For example, funds for breast cancer research are normally included in the appropriations bill for Labor, Health, and Human Services, Education and Related Agencies. Funds for such research have been added to the Defense Appropriations Bill in the past. This happened because the Subcommittee on Labor, Health and Human Services, Education and related agencies had used up its budget allocation. Thus, there are ways to get around the 302b allocations.

Appropriations bills are initiated in the House.

- The 13 Appropriations subcommittees hold hearings with witnesses from the departments and outside groups, review detailed budget justification materials prepared by the departments and agencies, and draft bills.
- The full Appropriations Committee then reviews and passes the bill, often with amendments.
- By law, the House may not begin to consider appropriations bills until May

15. (This is to provide time for passage of a budget resolution.)

- After passage by the House, usually with additional amendments, the bill is forwarded to the Senate for action.
- By June 30, House action on all appropriations bills is to be completed.

Senate committees conduct their own hearings, receive appeals to House bills from the Administration and prepare draft bills in anticipation of the House bill.

Continuing Resolutions

House and Senate action on some appropriations bills may not be completed by the start of the fiscal year. When this happens, Congress enacts a joint continuing resolution to provide appropriations authority for the affected agencies to continue operations at some specified level up to a specific date or until their regular appropriations are enacted. Like regular appropriations bills, continuing resolutions (called "CRs") must be presented to the President for approval or veto.

Presidential Action on Bills

The President may approve or veto bills.

A bill is approved when:

- the President has signed it or
- it has sat on the President's desk for 10 days while Congress is in session.

Most bills that become law are signed by the President. Some become law without signature when the President disagrees with some feature of a bill, but nevertheless strongly wants other provisions that are included in the bill.

A bill is vetoed when the President:

- returns it unsigned within 10 days to the Congress; or
- holds it, if Congress adjourns within 10 days.

If a bill is vetoed, the Congress can:

- override the veto by two-thirds vote of each house;
- rewrite the bill to make it acceptable to the President; or
- give up on that action.

Presidents and others have sought the authority to cancel specific provisions within a bill as a way to either end or reduce special interest pork barrel projects and the special tax benefits included in the bills passed by Congress. Because such authority involves constitutional issues, the Congress spent a considerable amount of time crafting legislation that might pass the constitutional test.

Such authority was given to the President in P.L. 104-130, which was signed into law on April 9, 1996, and went into effect on January 1, 1997. The act provided the following:

- The President can cancel provisions in bills or joint resolutions signed into law provided the cancellations will reduce the Federal budget deficit, not impair any essential government functions, and not harm the national interest.
- The action has to be taken and the Congress notified within five calendar days after the enactment of the law.
- The Congress then has five days to introduce a disapproval bill to override the cancellations.

The new authority was first used by President Clinton on August 11, 1997, when he canceled two items in the Taxpayer Relief Act of 1997 and one item in the Balanced Budget Act of 1997. Subsequently, he struck 78 provisions in nine FY 1998 appropriations bills. The savings in calendar year 1997 from the proposed cancellations totaled $855 million.

In February 1998, the District Court struck down the act as unconstitutional because, in the Court's view, it violates the Constitution's requirement that the president sign or veto bills as presented. The Supreme Court affirmed the District Court's judgement in June 1998. Thus, it is highly unlikely that the President will ever get such authority without a constitutional amendment.

Chapter 9
Budget Execution

Budget execution is what happens after an appropriations bill becomes law. Budget execution is how an agency administers its spending and collections authority.

Before any appropriated funds can be used, they must be apportioned to the organizational unit that will carry out the program.

Most of the funds will be spent as provided for in the appropriations and authorization acts. Sometimes, however, changes are desired to the budget authority (BA) provided in an act.

- The President may not want to spend the money for a specified program.
- The full amount of available funding may not be needed.
- It may not be feasible to use the funds immediately or even during the period of availability due to program delays.
- New requirements may develop, often of an emergency nature, that require funding not provided for in the act.

Depending on the situation, the President can propose to defer using the available authority or to rescind the authority. Some departments have the authority to transfer BA from one account or program to another in some circumstances.

Apportionment

Under current law, departments cannot obligate appropriated funds until they have released by the President. The process for releasing funds is called apportionment. The President must apportion each appropriation made to an Executive Branch department or agency.

- The President's authority to apportion funds is delegated to the Director of OMB.
- This process gives the President some control over the use of appropriations.

For example, apportioning funds by time period reduces the chance of a funding shortage before the end of the year.

Apportionment must be made by the later of: 20 days before the beginning of the fiscal year; or 30 days after enactment of the appropriation.

Funds not released for obligation are reserves, and such reserves must be reported to Congress.

Funds not required to carry out the objectives of the appropriation are to be recommended by the President for rescission.

Deferral

Deferral includes:

- withholding BA;
- delaying obligations; or
- other action that precludes obligation: for example, withholding the authority to obligate by contract in advance of appropriations,

Deferrals are permissible only under the following circumstances:

- to provide for contingencies;
- to achieve savings made possible by or through changes in requirements or greater efficiency of operations; or
- as specifically provided by law.

The President must send Congress a special message whenever BA provided for a specific purpose or project is deferred.

- The special message specifies the amount, account, department, project, length of deferral, reason, legal authority, budgetary effect, and any other relevant information.
- The deferral message may include one or more deferrals.

The Congress does not have to take any particular action in response to a deferral message.

Rescission

The President must send to the Congress a special message to rescind budget authority.
- A special message is required to reduce existing authority for any reason or if

BA provided for only one year is to be held in reserve for the whole year.

- The special message specifies the amount, account, department, project, reason, budgetary effect and any other relevant information.

For the rescission to occur, the Congress must pass a rescission bill.

- The bill can only rescind, in whole or in part, BA proposed for rescission in a special message from the President.
- The bill must be passed before the end of 45 calendar days of continuous session after submission of the rescission proposal.

If Congress does not pass a rescission bill, the BA proposed for rescission or reservation must be made available for obligation.

Funds made available for obligation due to lack of a rescission bill may not be proposed by the President for rescission again.

Congress can also initiate action on rescissions independently of the President. This is normally done in appropriations bills.

Special Procedures for Rescissions and Deferrals

The law contains detailed procedures for handling rescissions and deferrals (Title 2 U.S.C. Chapter 17B, Impoundment Control).

Each special message on deferrals and rescissions is transmitted to the House, the Senate and the Comptroller General (the head of the General Accounting Office) on the same day.

The Comptroller General provides the Congress an analysis of the facts.

If BA is reserved or deferred and the President has not transmitted a special message, the Comptroller General shall report that fact to Congress. The Comptroller General's report has the same effect as a special message from the President.

By the 10th of each month, the President must send the Congress a report listing all BA proposed for rescission, reservation, or deferral during that fiscal year.

If BA is not made available as required, the Comptroller General is to bring a civil action in the United States District Court for the District of Columbia.

- The Comptroller General must provide Congress an explanatory statement and wait for 25 calendar days of continuous session before taking legal action.
- The court is empowered to take action to make the BA available.

Reprogramming

The shifting of funds within or among appropriation accounts by an agency is called a "reprogramming."

- Reprogramming permits departments to respond to contingencies when they occur without having to go through the full congressional process.
- Appropriations bills provide guidance to the departments concerning reprogramming. While prior notification to, and approval of the Congress is not legally required, departments generally do not proceed with a reprogramming without concurrence from their principal committees.

Illustrative examples of Congressional reprogramming guidelines are shown in Table 9-1.

TABLE 9-1 EXAMPLES OF REPROGRAMMING AND TRANSFER AUTHORITY		
DEPARTMENT/LIMITATIONS	MAXIMUM AMOUNT ANY ACCOUNT CAN BE INCREASED	MAXIMUM FUNDS THAT CAN BE TRANSFERRED
COMMERCE		
-NO NEW PROGRAMS -NO DENIED PROGRAMS -NO PROGRAM INCREASE OVER $500K	10%	10% OF ACCOUNT
DEFENSE		
-OMB APPROVAL -FUNDS IN DOD BILL ONLY; NOT MILITARY CONSTRUCTION -NOTIFICATION -UNFORESEEN REQUIREMENTS	NO LIMIT	$1.65 BILLION
ENERGY		
-TO EMERGENCY PREPAREDNESS ONLY -UNFORSEEN NEEDS	NO LIMIT	NO LIMIT
HUD		
	2%	2% OF ACCOUNT
JUSTICE		
	10%	5% OF ACCOUNT
LABOR		
-TRANSFERS WITH TITLES I, II, OR III -PUBLIC HEALTH AND SOCIAL SERVICES EMERGENCY FUND NOT SUBJECT TO 3% LIMIT	3%	1% OF AMOUNT APPROPRIATED TO A TITLE
STATE		
-FUNDS IN COMMERCE, STATE, JUSTICE BILL ONLY	10%	5% OF ACCOUNT
TREASURY		
-NOTIFICATION -AMONG FUNDS FOR FEDERAL LAW ENFORCEMENT TRAINING CENTER, FINANCIAL SERVICES ENFORCEMENT NETWWORK, BATF, CUSTOMS, AND SECRET SERVICE -AMONG FUNDS FOR DEPARTMENTAL OFFICES, OFFICE OF INSPECTOR GENERAL, FINANCIAL MANAGEMENT SERVICE, BUREAU OF PUBLIC DEBT	2%	2% OF ACCOUNT

Chapter 10
The Regulatory Process

Federal agencies should promulgate only such regulations as are required by law, are necessary to interpret the law or are made necessary by compelling public need, to protect or improve the health and safety of the public, the environment, and the well-being of the American people.

Executive Order 12866

The Federal Government issues regulations that affect the public in much the same way as government spending and taxes. These regulations affect every citizen, business, and state and local government. They also cost a lot of money. A study by the Office of Management and Budget (OMB) estimated that Federal regulations cost the nation between $170 billion and $230 billion annually, almost 10 percent as much as is collected in taxes. (OMB report to Congress on the Costs and Benefits of Federal Regulations, 1998). About 70% of this cost is related to environmental regulations.

The process of developing and executing Federal regulation has proved to be complicated, costly, and inefficient. Several efforts have been made to streamline the process and to make it more open, efficient, and responsive to the public. The most recent example is the Clinton Administration's reform of the regulatory review process. The new process limits OMB reviews to "significant" regulatory policies, enhances public disclosure, increases public access to the regulatory decision-making process, and imposes time limits on each step of the process. Though these measures have had a positive effect, Federal regulatory procedure continues to be burdensome, expensive, and little-understood.

History of Regulatory Reform

Virtually every presidential administration beginning in the 1970s and continuing to date has promulgated methods designed to evaluate and improve the effectiveness of the regulatory system. These procedures were intended to eliminate cumbersome and time consuming reviews, and to ensure that the regulations were cost-effective.

- Nixon administration. A "Quality of Life Review" program focused on ensuring that environmental regulations minimized the government's burden on business.
- Ford Administration. President Ford issued an Executive Order requiring government agencies to prepare inflation impact statements prior to issuing costly new regulations. The Executive Order specified that a regulation would not be inflationary unless its costs to society exceeded the benefits produced. As a result, a "major" regulatory action was defined as one having an annual impact on the economy of over $100 million, a definition adopted by the next four Administrations.
- Carter Administration. This administration centralized review of new regulations in OMB's Regulatory Analysis Review Group and required a detailed analysis for every "major" rule before it could be issued.
- Reagan Administration. President Reagan issued an Executive Order that expanded OMB's role in overseeing and monitoring the regulatory impact assessment process, and designated OMB's Office of Information and Regulatory Affairs (OIRA) as responsible for centralized review. Additionally, agencies were required to review their existing regulations to determine which ones could be withdrawn or scaled back.
- Bush Administration. President Bush continued the regulatory review program established by the Reagan Administration.

Notwithstanding these attempts by previous administrations to grapple with regulatory issues, when President Clinton took office, it was widely agreed that further improvement was necessary.

Executive Order NO. 12866

The latest reform effort is that undertaken by President Clinton in Executive Order No. 12866, "Regulatory Planning and Review." Executive Order No. 12866 was part of his Administration's "Reinventing Government" initiative, the National Performance Review (NPR). The Executive Order requires agencies to assess all regulatory costs and benefits with a view toward developing better regulatory decision-making. The Executive Order reaffirms the legitimacy of centralized review within OMB of significant regulatory actions. Additionally, the Executive Order increases the visibility of the regulatory process by requiring that all written communications used in the process be placed in a public docket of the rulemaking agency for public review.

Role of the Office of Management and Budget

The OMB provides oversight of the regulatory activities of executive branch agencies. OMB provides guidance to the agencies and assists the President, Vice President, and other regulatory policy advisors in regulatory planning and in reviews of individual regulations. This ensures that agency rulemaking is consistent with laws, presidential priorities, and the principles stated in the Executive Order.

Within OMB, the Office of Information and Regulatory Affairs (OIRA) has oversight responsibility over regulatory matters. OIRA's centralized review is focused on regulations classified as "economically significant," (an annual affect on the economy of $100 million or greater), or "significant" because they affect other agencies' actions, have federal budgetary impact, or raise significant legal or policy issues.

Regulatory Policy Officers and Regulatory Working Group

Two interrelated entities created by Executive Order No. 12866 are the Regulatory Policy Officer (RPO) and the Regulatory Working Group (RWG). The RPO is a designated executive-level official at an agency who serves as the agency's representative to the RWG. The RWG coordinates regulatory activities that may affect more than one agency; provides a forum for agencies to exchange ideas concerning regulatory decision making and to discuss the best practices for development of effective regulations. The RWG meets at least quarterly and is chaired by an OIRA Administrator.

Intra-agency Review

Pursuant to Executive Order No. 12866, agencies are required to review their significant regulations periodically to determine whether they are burdensome, consistent with Presidential priorities and regulatory principles, cost-effective, and achieve their intended benefits.

Public Disclosure

A primary objective of the Executive Order is to enhance the accountability of the regulatory review process through increased public participation and increased public access to the information used in the formulation of regulations. A publicly-available list is maintained at OIRA, and updated daily, which describes all regulations currently under review by agency, title, date received, and the completion date of review. Additionally, a list of all meetings and conversations between the public and Congress pertaining to a regulatory action are on file. Once a regulation is published in the Federal Register, all draft regulations, economic analyses, and documents exchanged between OIRA and an agency are made available to the public.

Review Process for Significant Regulations

A main objective of Executive Order No. 12866 is to streamline the rulemaking process by preventing delays and focusing central review on the more significant regulations.

Development of the Annual Regulatory Program

Each year, the Vice President meets with agency representatives to learn their regulatory priorities and to coordinate the regulatory efforts on a government-wide basis for the upcoming year.

- For this review, agencies provide a draft Regulatory Plan to OIRA that describes the significant regulations they plan to issue during the current year. The plan includes a brief summary of intended regulatory action, the legal authority for action, and applicable deadlines.
- OIRA, the Vice President, OMB, and other advisors have 10 calendar days to review the plan. Their review focuses on whether the proposed actions will interfere with another agency's rules or established regulation, or if there is a potential conflict with administration priorities and objectives.
- After this process is completed, an annual Unified Regulatory Agenda is published that describes all of the significant regulatory actions under development for that year or the following year.

Public Comment Phase

When an agency finishes drafting a proposed regulation, it publishes the draft in the Federal Register and the public is given at least 60 days to submit comments.

Central Review of Significant Regulations

After the public comment phase is complete, the agency submits the draft rule to OIRA for evaluation of its significance. OIRA has 10 working days to review the regulation and to classify it as significant, economically significant, or not significant. If the proposed regulation is classified as significant (interferes with actions taken by another agency, raises legal or policy issues concerning legal mandates or Presidential priorities), or economically significant (impact of $100 million or greater on the economy), OIRA notifies the agency that the rule is subject to the central review process.

- Not significant. If the proposed rule is determined to be not significant it is not subject to further OIRA review. The agency will then use its internal review processes to complete the rulemaking process.
- Significant. If the proposed rule is determined to be significant, the issuing agency must justify the need for the regulatory action and how the action will address that need. The agency must develop a cost-benefit assessment including an explanation of how the proposed action avoids interference with state, local, and tribal governments in the exercise of their governmental functions.

- Economically Significant. If the proposed rule is determined to be economically significant, the agency must develop a cost-benefit assessment that analyzes the potential costs and benefits of the proposed action. In addition, the agency must provide an assessment of potential alternatives to the regulation and explain why the planned action is preferable.

OIRA Review

Once the agency has provided the required material for review, OIRA has 90 days for review. During this time, OIRA may make inquiries about any facts or circumstances concerning the regulatory action. If more time is needed for review, an extension of 30 calendar days may be given with the approval by the OMB Director and at the request of an agency official.

Every regulatory action that is returned to an agency for additional consideration must be accompanied with an explanation of the reason for its return. The agency head may then disagree or raise questions by submitting them in writing to the Administrator of OIRA.

After the draft regulation has been modified, it is returned to OIRA for further review. If no change is recorded on the conditions or facts of the regulatory action, OIRA has 45 days to complete its review. If OIRA determines that more consideration of the action by the issuing agency is needed, OIRA can return the proposal to the agency.

Public Disclosure

Once a final draft is approved by OIRA, all changes and correspondence that were made during the review process are then made available at the agency for public review. Records of meetings with members of Executive Branch personnel and others are made available for public review or inquiry in OIRA's public room.

Congressional Review

Prior to becoming a final rule, the Congress is given an opportunity to review the regulation. The issuing agency must provide Congress a copy and summary of the rule, the determination as whether it is a significant action, the effective date of the rule, and any relevant analyses.

The Congress has 60 days to disapprove the regulation. If the Congress takes no action in 60 days, the rule is final. The agency may publish the final regulation in the Federal Register before the end of the congressional review period provided the effective date is after the 60-day congressional review period.

The Congress can stop the regulation by passing a joint resolution of disapproval. The President can veto the resolution, and if either House of Congress fails to override the veto or takes no action within 30 session days of receiving the veto, the rule then takes effect.

An exception to the Congressional and review requirement occurs when the President notifies Congress that a particular rule addresses an imminent threat to the environment, to human health and/or safety, is necessary for national security, or necessary for the enforcement of criminal laws.

Publishing the Final Regulation

Upon the completion of Congressional Review, the rule is published in the Federal Register as a final rule. As previously stated, the agency may publish the regulation in the Federal Register before the end of the congressional review period provided the effective date is after the 60-day congressional review period. All information concerning changes within the regulatory action is made available to the public.

Future Plans

The FY 2000 President's Budget indicates that the Government needs better data and analysis to determine whether proposed regulations maximize social benefits while minimizing cost. According to the Budget, OMB is committed to assessing and improving its performance in ensuring that it is faithfully executing and managing applicable regulatory policy. It will continue to lead an inter-agency effort to raise the quality of analyses used in developing regulations by offering technical outreach programs and training sessions on using OMB's "Best Practices" on economic analysis.

OMB also plans to:

- continue to develop a database on benefits and costs of major rules, using consistent assumptions and better techniques to refine agency estimates of incremental costs and benefits; and
- develop appropriate methodologies to evaluate whether to reform or eliminate existing regulatory programs or their elements.

Chapter 11

Information Technology Management

Information technology is a key to improved performance in most agencies. Several steps have been taken to improve the government's performance in this critical area.

The first step was enactment of the Information Technology Management Reform Act (ITMRA), which went into effect in August 1996. Commonly referred to as the Clinger-Cohen Act, ITMRA was based on S. 946, introduced by then-Senator William Cohen (R-ME), and H.R. 1670, introduced by then-Representative William F. Clinger (R-PA). Its primary purpose was to reform the procurement and management of information technology within government agencies. The Brooks Act, which had provided legal guidance for the acquisition of information systems since 1965, was repealed.

A second important step has been recognition in the Executive Branch of the need for improved management of Information technology resources. This recognition resulted from the efforts of Vice President Gore's Reinvention initiative, the National Performance Review, and increased focus within the agencies on Information technology expenditures and the benefits possible from improved use of Information technology.

Need for Reform of Information System Acquisition

When it was passed, the Brooks Act was intended to promote fairness and competition in the federal government contracting for information technology products. Over the years, its provisions became more of an impediment to progress than a means for achieving economy and efficiency in the procurement of information systems. The Brooks Act did not address the main information technology problems, which were inadequate definition of agency information system needs, agency preference for custom-made products over "off-the-shelf" technologies; and the lengthy procurement process that often resulted in the acquisition of systems that were obsolete by the time they were delivered.

This inefficiency was not limited to information technology products. Many of the same problems also existed with the acquisition of other types of products. To address these problems, the government began to examine ways the agencies could:

- increase efficiency through the contracting out of certain functions;
- increase the freedom and speed with which acquisitions are made; and
- reduce costs through the purchase of commercial, off-the-shelf systems where applicable.

In 1991, Congress asked the Department of Defense (DOD) to review its acquisition system and to recommend improvements. After a series of budget reductions, DOD had already begun evaluating how to make defense acquisition more efficient. This study became a major resource for the National Performance Review (NPR) and a component of the Clinton Administration's efforts to reform the government-wide acquisition process.

Congress began looking with growing concern at the large expenditures being made on information technology systems. It was becoming increasingly apparent that in an era of smaller government and budget reductions, the successful use of information technology offered the prospect of achieving greater results with lower expenditures.

Subsequently, Congress enacted a series of reform measures that addressed government performance, federal procurement, and information management. These included: the Government Performance and Results Act, the Federal Acquisition Streamlining Act; the Federal Acquisition Reform Act; and the Information Technology Management Reform Act.

Information Technology Management Reform Act

The intent of ITMRA was to shift management attention toward the potential outcome that successful use of information technology procurement and management could achieve and away from procedures and process, which were the focus of the Brooks Act.

The new Act defines Information technology as:

- Any equipment or interconnected system or subsystem of equipment that is used in the automatic acquisition, storage, manipulation, management, movement, control, display, switching, interchange, transmission, or reception of data or information by the executive agency.

Under ITMRA:

- information technology management is to be linked to the agency mission and budget formulation;

- agency management is made accountable for information technology projects by requiring the development of performance measures that are tied to the agency's Strategic Plan;
- authority for acquisition of computer resources, which previously was centralized in the General Services Administration, is placed in the individual agencies; and
- the Director of the Office of Management and Budget (OMB) is responsible for oversight of information technology management.

Each agency head is to take the following actions:

- design and implement a management process for information technology acquisition;
- integrate the information technology management process with agency processes for budget and program management;
- develop goals for improving the efficiency and effectiveness of Information technology use and where appropriate, the delivery of information technology related services to the general public;
- measure the success of information technology in supporting agency programs;
- ensure proper information technology security policies; and,
- appoint a qualified senior-level Chief Information Officer (CIO).

The Act encouraged the incremental acquisition of information technology systems within government agencies, encouraged the acquisition of commercial off-the-shelf products and systems, and allowed for pilot programs to test new approaches to information technology acquisition. Additionally, it eliminated the authorities of the General Services Board of Contract Appeals to hear protests regarding information technology and allocated this power to the General Services Administration.

For purposes of national security, ITMRA has a limited application with regard to critical national security systems.

Executive Order No. 13011

Following enactment of ITMRA and prior to its going into effect, President Clinton issued Executive Order No. 13011, which states the government's vision for managing information technology and provides direction for implementation of the Act.

The Executive Order requires government agencies to:

- refocus information technology management to support directly their strategic missions, including rethinking the way they perform their functions before investing in Information technology to support that work;

- establish clear accountability for information resources management activities by creating the position of Chief Information Officer (CIO);
- cooperate with other agencies in the use of information technology to improve the productivity of federal programs and to promote government-wide infrastructure compatibility;
- expand the skill and career development opportunities of information technology professionals.

In addition, the Executive Order ordered the creation of a Chief Information Officers Council (CIO Council), a Government Information Technology Services Board, and an Information Technology Resources Board to facilitate implementation of ITMRA.

Chief Information Officers Council

The CIO Council is an interagency forum for discourse on information technology practices, uses, training, and performance. It's functions are tasked to:

- develop recommendations for overall federal information technology management policy, procedures, and standards;
- share experiences and ideas, including work process redesign and development of performance measures;
- identify opportunities for cooperation in using information resources;
- assess the hiring, training, and professional development needs of the government with respect to information resources management;
- make recommendations to the agencies and to OMB concerning the government-wide strategic plan required by the Paperwork Reduction Act of 1995; and
- seek the views of the Chief Financial Officers Council, the Information Technology Resources Board, Federal Procurement Council, industry, academia, and State and local governments.

The CIO Council is composed of the CIO and Deputy CIOs of all federal agencies and two representatives each from the Office of Information and Regulatory Affairs; the Office of Federal Financial Management; the Office of Federal Procurement Policy; the Office of Science and Technology Policy; the Government Information Technology Services Board; and, the Information Technology Services Board.

The Chair of the CIO Council is the Deputy Director for Management of OMB and the Vice Chair, an agency CIO, is elected on a rotating basis.

Government Information Technology Services Board

The purpose of the Government Information Technology Services Board (the Services Board) is to ensure continued implementation of the information technology recommendations of the National Performance Review and to identify and promote the development of innovative technologies, standards, and practices among the agencies, state and local governments, and the private sector. Additionally, the Services Board is to assist in creating opportunities for interagency cooperation, developing shared government-wide information infrastructure services, and developing guidelines for Federal information systems.

The Board is composed of government personnel with proven expertise or accomplishments in appropriate fields. The Chair is elected by the board.

Information Technology Resources Board

The mission of the Information Technology Resources Board is to provide independent assessments to agency heads and OMB concerning the development, acquisition, and management of selected major information systems.

Composed of knowledgeable individuals from executive branch agencies, the Board is to:

* review, upon agency or OMB request, specific information systems proposed or under development and to make recommendations on their status or next steps;
* publicize the lessons learned based on those reviews; and
* consult with experts in academia, industry, and government, as appropriate.

Agency Chief Information Officer

The Paperwork Reduction Act of 1995 (PRA) required that a senior agency official be designated within each agency for oversight of agency information resources management. ITMRA goes a step further by requiring that each agency establish a CIO position.

The CIO's mission is to facilitate the development, implementation, and maintenance of the agency's information technology architecture, and to ensure effective operation of all information resources management processes. The CIO is also charged with promoting effective agency operations by implementing budget-linked capital planning for, and performance-based management of, information technology systems.

The duties of the CIO are to:

- monitor and evaluate the performance of information technology programs on the basis of performance measurements, and advise the head of the agency on the status of programs and projects;
- annually assess the requirements for personnel knowledge and skill in the area of information management;
- annually assess the level at which these requirements are met;
- develop strategy and specific plans for hiring, training, and professional development in the area of information technology management; and,
- submit an annual report to the head of the agency on progress made in improving information resources management.

Although each agency makes its own determination of the CIO's organizational placement, the CIO must report directly to the agency head; participate in agency planning and budget deliberations; be involved in all work-process redesign directly related to information technology investment; and develop information technology program performance measures.

Agencies may create CIOs for the major subdivisions or bureaus of the agency and appoint deputy CIOs to assist with information technology management.

Since the creation of the CIO position, job turnover has been a problem. To date, three agencies — the Navy, Department of Housing and Urban Development, and the United State Agency for International Development — have already had resignations of permanent CIOs. NASA, DOD, and GSA have witnessed the departure of acting CIOs.

The job turnover has been credited to several factors, including an overwhelming workload and lack of congressional oversight. Fifteen of the twenty-seven agencies have combined the CIO duties with other responsibilities. Several have combined the CIO and Chief Financial Officer (CFO) roles into one position.

The Role of OMB

With regard to information resources, ITMRA requires the Director of OMB to:

- exercise capital planning control;
- promote improvement of federal programs addressing information technology;
- develop a process for tracking and evaluating the risks and results of major capital investments in information systems;
- compare and disseminate the results of agencies' uses of information technology;

- monitor the development and implementation of training and for executive personnel;
- review policy associated information technology acquisition and coordinate its development;
- assess alternatives for managing information technology; and
- oversee the development and implementation by the Secretary of Commerce of standards and guidelines pertaining to federal computer systems.

In order to carry out its responsibilities under ITMRA, OMB has issued guidance in the form of memoranda and circulars to Executive Departments concerning the position of CIO, the role of the General Services Board of Contract Appeals, CIO Education and Training, evaluating Information Technology Investments, funding Information Systems Investments, and capital programming.

Major Information Technology Investments in the FY 2000 Budget

The President's budget for FY 2000 identifies 48 information technology systems costing $3.3 billion in FY 2000 as major investments. All are expected to provide important program performance benefits. (Table 11-1)

TABLE 11-1 MAJOR INFORMATION TECHNOLOGY INVESTMENTS IN THE FY 2000 BUDGET			
DEPARTMENT/AGENCY	NUMBER OF SYSTEMS	FY 2000 REQUEST ($MILLIONS)	PERFORMANCE BENEFITS
AGRICULTURE	4	213	"ONE-STOP SERVICE" FOR FARMERS, FOOD SAFETY, IMPROVED LAND USE
AID	1	42	IMPROVE MANAGEMENT OF BILATERAL DEVELOPMENT
COMMERCE	2	341	IMPROVE WEATHER FORECASTS, REDUCE ERRORS & COST OF 2000 CENSUS
DEFENSE	3	235	TIMELY & SECURE MESSAGE
EDUCATION	7	501	IMPROVE GRANT AND LOAN SERVICES AND COLLECTION ON DEFAULTED LOANS
ENERGY	2	44	IMPROVE FINANCIAL MANAGEMENT AND COMMUNICATIONS
HEALTH & HUMAN SERVICES	3	67	IMPROVE NEW DRUG AND MEDICAL DELIVERY AND LOCATING NON-CUSTODIAL PARENTS
HOUSING & URBAN DEVELOPMENT	3	70	IMPROVE FINANCIAL MANAGEMENT AND CUSTOMER SERVICE
INTERIOR	4	64	IMPROVE ACCESS TO LAND INFORMATION AND ALLOCATION OF INDIAN TRUST INCOME
JUSTICE	3	100	REDUCING TIME FOR FINGERPRINT INFORMATION, PROMOTE SHARING OF INVESTIGATIVE DATA
LABOR	1	6	IMPROVE PROCESSING OF PRIVATE PENSION DATA
STATE	1	236	IMPROVE DELIVERY OF DIPLOMATIC INFORMATION
TRANSPORTATION	3	432	IMPROVE AIR TRAFFIC CONTROL
TREASURY	1	200	IMPROVE SECURE DATA TRANSMISSION
VETERANS AFFAIRS	2	364	AUTOMATE VETERAN RECORDS AND IMPROVE HEALTH CARE
EPA	1	8	IMPROVE EPA AND PUBLIC ACCESS TO DATA ON TOXIC CHEMICALS
NASA	1	187	IMPROVE CAPABILITY FOR HANDLING LARGE QUANTITIES OF DAATA
NUCLEAR REGULATORY COMMISSION	2	3	REFORM WORK PROCESSES
INTERAGENCY	4	149	PROVIDE 50% INCREASE IN MOBILE RADIOS
TOTAL	48	$3,262	

Chapter 12

Opportunities and Challenges

The projected budget surpluses presents many opportunities. Many challenges, however, remain that have to be addressed.

The budget presented by the President makes several optimistic assumptions about future funding of discretionary programs.

- Reductions, now undefined in program terms, are required in the budget authority for some domestic programs to provide funding for high priority administration initiatives and to remain within the discretionary limits for fiscal years 2001 and 2002. Functions in which real reductions will be required based on the President's Budget include International Affairs, General Science and Technology, Natural Resources and Environment, and Agriculture.

- The Department of Defense budget for 2000 and beyond assumes that significant cost savings will result from planned reforms in operating activities, especially commercial type activities and by additional base closures. If those savings are not realized, the Department will not be able to meet its procurement and force structure objectives.

- The budget assumes that Congress will agree to increase discretionary spending.

- Further complicating the situation is the possibility that the economy will not perform over the next five years as assumed in the budget, or that the projections may prove to be inaccurate. In the past, projections have at times been far off the mark. For FY 1995, a surplus of $69 billion projected when the Budget Agreement of 1990 was passed proved to be $233 billion off the mark when the actual FY 1995 results were in and a deficit of $164 billion was reported. For FY 1997 the deficit dropped from a projected level of $125 billion in February to only $22 billion eight months later. For FY 1998 a deficit of $10 billion was projected in February 1998, the actual result 8 months later was a surplus of $70 billion. This is not to say the projected surpluses will not occur. Rather, it is to urge caution in putting too much credence in long-term budget projections, given past results on relatively short-term forecasting. Small changes in the economic factors can result in significant savings in the surplus and deficit in a very short time period.

In addition, there are issues under consideration last year that still have to be resolved. These include the following:

- resolving long-term solvency problems facing some Trust Funds, especially Social Security and Medicare,
- responding to complaints that taxes are too high and that the tax system is broken,
- deciding how to use more of the funds being collected for specific uses for their intended purposes without major change to the budget balance,
- how to provide adequate resources for high priority programs such as national defense, health, environment, and education within appropriations caps that are declining in real purchasing power, and
- how to improve government planning and results through GPRA.

Solvency of Medicare and Social Security Trust Funds

The long-term solvency of the Medicare and Social Security Trust Funds requires attention. This will be a significant budget issue in Congress this year.

- Considerable progress was made in 1997 on Medicare reforms. Those actions reportedly extended the life of the Medicare Trust Fund by ten years. The budget proposes to set aside 15% of the projected surplus to ensure the vitality of the Medicare Trust Fund for the next 20 years.
- The Social Security Trust Fund is projected to continue collecting more money than it spends until 2012. At that time, spending will begin exceeding receipts and the reserves in the fund will be depleted by 2032. The budget proposes to set aside 62% of the projected surpluses over the next 15 years to keep Social Security viable through 2055. An additional 12% would be set aside to establish universal savings accounts.

Taxes

Taxes were reduced as part of the 1997 budget agreement. The projected budget surpluses are adding to the pressure for across-the-board tax cuts. As pointed out earlier, government receipts as a percentage of GDP are at high levels. Although there appears to be general support for a simpler tax system, no proposals have been put forth yet that would meet the objectives of simplicity and fairness, and provide incentives for actions that are considered good for the nation, such as charitable contributions and home ownership.

The President's Budget does not propose general tax cuts. Rather, it would use the surplus for Medicare, Social Security, individual savings accounts, to increase discretionary spending, and for selected tax reductions targeted for certain groups of people such as stay-at-home parents.

Some Taxes Are Being Diverted

Some taxes are being collected to pay for certain services such as air transportation but the intended services are not being provided.

The tax receipts to pay for the work are deposited in trust funds to keep them separate from general tax revenues. Expenditures to accomplish the needed work are to be made from the Trust Funds. The expenditures, however, must be included in appropriations acts in which they compete for funding with other programs under the discretionary caps. The difference between the taxes collected and actual appropriations for the special programs is being used either as a source of funds to pay for other programs or as a source of cash for deficit reduction. In several cases, the budget does not reflect any plans for using the accumulated balances in the Trust Funds to do work in the designated area.

For example, the government assesses a fee on power companies that use nuclear fuel to cover the cost of disposing of the toxic wastes. Supporting information provided with the FY 2000 budget shows annual collections of $600 million but spending of only $200 million each year. That annual profit plus interest on the balance will cause the balance in the Nuclear Waste Disposal Fund to increase from $7.3 billion in 1998 to over $13 billion in 2004. Since the fee levels are supposed to be set on the basis of work to be performed, some needed work apparently is not being performed or the fees are set too high.

Similar actions are occurring with other Trust Funds. For example, the balance in the Airport and Airway Trust Fund is projected to increase from $9 billion in 1998 to almost $21 billion in 2004.

Discretionary Programs

The existing legal caps on discretionary appropriations through 2002 require reductions in the real level of resources for government programs. Unless the caps are increased, government-wide reductions will be substantial, especially if defense is to be increased. Those reductions are not yet specified. The budget proposes to use 11 percent of the projected surpluses over the next 15 years to increase the discretionary caps for spending on defense, education, and other domestic needs. Even with that increase, real cuts will be required in other areas.

Government Performance and Results Act (GPRA)

Over the past two years, there has been considerable activity and focus on the development of strategic plans and performance goals for each agency of government. These plans can be a useful way for the agencies to state their goals and objectives, lay out performance measures, and build public confidence in their activities. The first effort was positive, but more work is needed. Examination of agency plans leads to the conclusion that some of their objectives and measures could use further refinement. GPRA provides an opportunity for the agencies to present their stories in terms that the public can understand. That also is the challenge for the agencies. The strategic plans will become especially useful when they become strategy documents for the departments. That is the case for the Department of Defense, which produced its Quadrennial Defense Review of defense strategy in a form that permitted it to be adopted as the department's strategic plan, and the basis for measuring departmental performance.

Conclusion

Though the federal budget receives attention in the press only infrequently, often highlighting acrimony between the Congress and the President, work on the budget demands the attention, effort, and cooperation of the Administration and the Congress throughout the year.

The creation of the federal budget is not glamorous, but it is where the nation expresses itself in terms of programs and priorities. The consequences of actions taken today will have a profound effect on the economic security and physical well-being of future generations.

Chapter 13
Glossary of Budget Terms

This glossary provides an extensive list of terms used in federal budgeting and in the budget process. The emphasis in developing this list is on providing understandable, common-sense definitions.

ACCRUED EXPENDITURES - Charges during a given period that reflect liabilities incurred for: (a) service performed by employees, contractors, and others; (b) goods and other property received; and, (c) amounts becoming owed under programs for which no current service or performance is required, such as annuities and other benefit payments. Expenditures accrue regardless of when cash payments are made.

ACTIVITY/PROGRAM BUDGET - The budget for a specific and/or discrete program or program activity performed by a governmental unit to accomplish its objectives. For example, the budget developed for food inspection is managed as an activity performed in the discharge of the health function.

ACTUAL EXPENDITURE(S) - Actual spending for a prior fiscal year, as opposed to a budget estimate.

ADVANCE APPROPRIATION - Budget authority provided in an appropriation act that will become available in a fiscal year after the fiscal year for which the appropriation is passed. The amount is not included in the budget totals for the year in which the appropriation is enacted but it is included in the budget totals for the fiscal year in which the amount will become available for obligation.

AGENCY - The governmental entity for which there is a total allocation of budgetary resources; often used interchangeably with Department. There is no single definition of the term agency. Any given definition usually relates to specific legislation. Generally, an "executive agency" means any executive branch department, independent commission, board, bureau, office, or other establishment of the Federal Government, including independent regulatory commissions and boards. (The term sometimes includes the municipal government of the District of Columbia).

ALLOTMENT - An authorization by the head (or other authorized employee) of an agency to his/her subordinates to incur obligations within a specified amount. The amount allotted by an agency cannot exceed the amount apportioned by the Office of Management and Budget (OMB). Exceeding an allotment results in an anti-deficiency violation.

ALLOWANCES - Amounts included in the President's budget request or projections to cover possible additional proposals, such as statutory pay increases and contingencies for relatively uncontrollable programs and other requirements. Allowances are also used to indicate savings required to meet budget totals. As used by Congress in the concurrent resolution on the budget, allowances represent a special functional classification designed to include amounts to cover possible requirements, such as civilian pay raises and contingencies. Allowances remain undistributed until they become firm, then they are distributed to the appropriate functional classification(s).

ANNUAL AUTHORIZATION - Legislation that authorizes appropriations for a single fiscal year. Programs with annual authorizations must be authorized each year and for a definite sum of money.

ANNUAL PERFORMANCE PLAN - A plan required by the Government Performance and Results Act that shows the outcomes and outputs expected during a specific year at the proposed budget level.

ANNUAL PERFORMANCE REPORT - A report required by the Government Performance and Results Act that compares the actual performance to (1) the performance proposed in the budget and (2) the performance expected at enacted appropriations levels, and that explains the variance and possible corrective measures.

ANTIDEFICIENCY ACT - The law that prohibits the incurring of obligations or expenditures (outlays) in excess of the amounts available in appropriations or funds and the amounts authorized to be obligated in apportionments.

APPEALS PROCESS - The process for seeking a change to a budget decision within an Agency/Department or the OMB. In recent years the incentive to Department and Agency Heads is to resolve appeals at the OMB Program Associate Director levels rather than to plead a case to the Director or President. Under the reinventing government initiative, agencies have greater flexibility to set their own priorities, so long as they are generally consistent with the President's priorities and do not violate budget scorekeeping requirements.

APPORTIONMENT - A distribution made by OMB of amounts available for obligation, including budgetary reserves established pursuant to law, in an appropriation or fund account. Apportionments divide amounts available for obligation by specific time periods (usually quarters), activities, projects, objects, or a combination thereof. The amounts so apportioned limit the amount of obligations that may be incurred. In apportioning any account, some funds may be reserved to provide for contingencies or to effect savings, pursuant to the Antideficiency Act; or may be proposed for deferral or rescission pursuant to the Impoundment Control Act of 1974. The apportionment process is intended to prevent accruing obligations in a manner that would require deficiency or supplemental appropriations and to achieve the most effective and economical use of the funds available for obligation.

APPROPRIATION - An appropriation generally provides funds for one year only. For some capital investment programs, the appropriation act may make the funds available for more than one year. Appropriations represent limitations of amounts that agencies may obligate for certain activities during the period of time specified in the respective appropriation acts. Several types of appropriations are not counted as budget authority, since they do not provide authority to incur additional obligations. Examples of these are: appropriations to liquidate contract authority; appropriations to reduce outstanding debt; and appropriations for refunds of receipts.

APPROPRIATION ACT - A statute, initially drafted under the jurisdiction of the House and Senate Committees on Appropriations, that generally provides authorization for Federal agencies to incur obligations and to make payments out of the Treasury for specified purposes. An appropriation act generally follows enactment of authorizing legislation which permits, but doesn't require, subsequent appropriations.

Currently, there are 13 regular annual appropriation acts. From time to time, Congress passes supplemental appropriations. Generally, funding in appropriation acts is considered "discretionary".

APPROPRIATION ACCOUNT/FUND ACCOUNT - A summary account established in the Treasury for each appropriation and/or fund.

APPROPRIATION (EXPENDITURE), RECEIPT, AND FUND ACCOUNTS - Accounts used by the Federal Government from which expenditures can be made or receipts deposited. Some accounts are used only for accounting purposes, e.g., transfer appropriation accounts, foreign currency accounts, receipt clearing accounts, and deposit fund accounts.

APPROPRIATIONS LIMITATION - A statutory restriction in appropriations acts that establishes the maximum or minimum amount that may be obligated or expended for specified purposes.

AUTHORIZING COMMITTEE - A standing committee of the House or Senate with legislative jurisdiction over the subject matter of laws that set up or continue the operations of Federal programs or agencies. It can propose direct spending authority to fund programs or make funding subject to subsequent appropriations action. An authorizing committee also has jurisdiction in those instances where backdoor authority is provided in the substantive legislation.

AUTHORIZING LEGISLATION - Substantive legislation that establishes or continues the operation of a Federal program or agency either indefinitely or for a specific period of time or sanctions a particular type of obligation or expenditure within a program. Authorizing legislation is normally a prerequisite for appropriations. It may place a limit on the amount of budget authority to be included in appropriations acts or it may authorize the appropriation of "such sums as may be necessary." Authorizing legislation may provide authority to incur debts, or to mandate payment to particular persons or political subdivisions of the country. Authorizing legislation is usually, but not always, drafted by Authorizing Committees.

BACKDOOR AUTHORITY - Budget authority provided in legislation outside the normal (Appropriations Committee) appropriations process. The most common forms of backdoor authority are authority to borrow (also called borrowing authority or authority to spend debt receipts) and contract authority. Section 401 of the Congressional Budget and Impoundment Control Act of 1974 (2 U.S.C. 651) specifies certain limits on the use of backdoor authority.

BALANCED BUDGET - A fiscal year budget in which receipts are equal to or greater than outlays.

BALANCES OF BUDGET AUTHORITY - Amounts of budget authority that have not been outlayed. Unobligated balances are amounts that have not been obligated and remain available for the following year.

BASELINE - A benchmark projection that generally reflects the receipts, outlays, and deficit or surplus that will result if all current laws are continued through the period covered by the budget. Congress uses the CBO baseline to conduct its analysis of budget issues and for budget debate with the Executive Branch. The baseline reflects budget trends using expected inflation rates, provisions of law and other factors. The baseline has been used for measuring expenditure reductions in the reconciliation process and for projecting future budget conditions.

BORROWING AUTHORITY - Statutory authority that permits a Federal agency to incur obligations and to make payments for specified purposes out of borrowed monies.

BREACH - The amount by which new discretionary budget authority or outlays within a category of discretionary appropriations for a fiscal year exceeds the legal cap for that year.

BUDGET - The Budget of the United States Government that sets forth the President's comprehensive financial plan and indicates the President's priorities for the Federal Government. (See President's Budget).

BUDGET AMENDMENT - Revision to a pending appropriations request.

BUDGET AUTHORITY - Authority becoming available during the year to enter into obligations that will result in immediate or future outlays of Federal Government funds. The basic forms of budget authority are appropriations, authority to borrow, contract authority, and authority to spend certain receipts. Budget authority may be classified by the period of availability (1-year, multiple-year, no-year), by the type of congressional action (current or permanent), or by the manner of determining the amount available (definite or indefinite).

BUDGET BASELINE - This estimate assumes that Federal spending and revenue levels based on current policies will continue unchanged in the upcoming fiscal year. For revenue levels and entitlement program spending, the budget baseline assumes continuation of current laws. For discretionary spending, the baseline assumes an adjustment for inflation (GDP deflator) added to the previous year's discretionary spending levels. The baseline includes funds to cover a federal pay comparability raise.

BUDGET DEFICIT - The amount by which the Government's budget outlays exceed its budget receipts for a given fiscal year.

BUDGET EXAMINER - Standard position title for employee of OMB responsible for the oversight of program implementation, policy formulation, legislative formulation, clearance of testimony and other Congressional submissions and development of the President's Budget for a specific set of programs or appropriation accounts.

BUDGET ESTIMATES - Estimates of budget authority, outlays, receipts, or other budget measures that cover the current and future budget years, as reflected in the President's budget and budget updates.

BUDGET HEARINGS - Congressional opportunity to question Executive Branch and other witnesses about program needs, costs, and results, to challenge or support decisions reached within the Executive Branch and to build a record for proposed changes to the President's Budget.

BUDGET HIGHLIGHTS - A summary of significant proposals included in a Department/Agency Budget submission which is prepared in advance of the Congressional justification. The timing of the document is simultaneous with the transmittal of the President's Budget.

BUDGET RESOLUTION - See Concurrent Resolution on the Budget.

BUDGET SURPLUS - The amount by which the Government's receipts exceed its outlays for a given fiscal year.

BUDGET TARGETS (GUIDANCE) - Letter from the Director of OMB which sets forth agency budget ceilings for the upcoming budget formulation cycle. OMB transmits budget policy letters to the Executive Branch Departments and Agencies or provides guidance and directives to Heads of Departments at Cabinet meetings.

BUDGET TESTIMONY - Elaboration and defense of the President's budget generally by members of the cabinet and other political officers of the Administration.

BUDGET TOTALS - The totals for budget authority, outlays, and receipts included in the budget. Some presentations in the budget distinguish on-budget totals from off-budget totals. On-budget totals reflect the transactions of all Federal Government entities except those excluded from the budget totals by law. Off-budget totals reflect the transactions of Government entities that are excluded from the on-budget totals by law. Currently excluded are the social security trust funds (Federal Old -Age and Survivors Insurance and Federal Disability Insurance Trust Funds) and the Postal Service Fund. The on-and off-budget totals are combined to derive a total for Federal activity.

BUDGET UPDATES - Amendments to, or revisions in, budget authority requests, estimated outlays, deficit estimates and estimated receipts for the ensuing fiscal year. The President is required to transmit an mid-session review update to Congress by July 15 of each year. However, the President may also submit budget updates at other times during the fiscal year.

BUDGET YEAR - The fiscal year for which a budget is proposed.

BUDGETARY RESERVES - Portions of budgetary resources set aside (withheld from apportionment) by the OMB by authority of the Antideficiency Act (31 U.S.C. 1512) and the Budget Impoundment and Control Act of 1974 to (a) provide for contingencies, (b) achieve savings made possible by or through changes in requirements or greater efficiency of operations, or (c) as specified by law.

BUDGETARY RESOURCES - Budgetary resources comprise new budget authority, unobligated balances of budget authority, direct spending authority, and obligation limitations.

CAP - Term commonly used to refer to legal limits on the budget authority and outlays for each fiscal year for each of the discretionary appropriations categories. A sequester is required if an appropriation for a category causes a breach in the cap.

CAPABILITY STATEMENT - Response to direct Congressional inquiries concerning a program's capability to spend resources above the President's request.

CAPITAL BUDGET - Budget providing for separate financing of (a) capital or investment expenditures and (b) current or operating expenditures. Investments in capital assets generally would be excluded from calculations of the budget surplus or deficit. The Federal Government has never had a capital budget in the sense of financing capital or investment-type programs separately from current expenditures.

CATEGORIES OF DISCRETIONARY APPROPRIATIONS - See Spending Caps.

CBO BASELINE - CBO version of a current services baseline, which is generally used as the baseline for the Concurrent Resolution on the Budget.

COLLECTIONS - Amounts received by the Federal Government during the fiscal year. Collections are classified into two major categories:

• BUDGET RECEIPTS - Collections from the public based on the Government's exercise of its sovereign powers, from payments by participants in certain voluntary Federal social insurance premiums, and court fines, certain licenses, and deposits of earnings by the Federal Reserve System. Gifts and contributions (as distinguished from payments for services or cost-sharing deposits by State and local governments) are also counted as budget receipts. Budget receipts are compared with the total outlays in calculating the budget surplus or deficit.

• OFFSETTING COLLECTIONS - Collections from Government accounts or from transactions with the public that are of a business-type or market-oriented nature. They are classified into two major categories: (a) collections credited to appropriation or fund accounts, and (b) offsetting receipts (i.e., amounts deposited in receipt accounts). In general, the "collections credited to appropriation or fund accounts" can be used to pay for program costs, whereas funds in "receipt accounts" cannot be used without being appropriated. Offsetting collections are deducted from disbursements in calculating total outlays.

COMMITTEE ALLOCATION - Recommended appropriation level following Congressional Subcommittee and full Committee action.

COMMITTEE HEARINGS - Forum in which Executive Branch witnesses (generally political officers within the Administration) defend the President's budget proposals and the members of the Committee (often prompted by the staff) build the record that justifies their position on the President's proposals.

COMMITTEE MARK-UP - The proposed Congressional changes to the President's budget following Committee hearings.

COMMITTEE PRINT - Draft Committee action following markup.

COMMITTEE REPORT - A report contains directives, instructions and Congressional reasoning/intent, which accompanies enacted appropriations and which supports and clarifies the appropriations. While not legally binding on the Executive Branch, most political and program manager's view report language as binding.

CONCURRENT RESOLUTION ON THE BUDGET (Budget Resolution) - A resolution passed by both Houses of Congress, but not requiring the signature of the

President, setting forth or revising the Congressional budget for the United States Government for one or more fiscal years. The resolution, due April 15, sets spending targets for the entire government, and subdivides them into Congressional Committee allocations. It is to be passed by Congress before appropriations bills move forward.

CONFEREES - Congressional members from both houses appointed to resolved differences between House and Senate versions of legislation.

CONFERENCE COMMITTEE - Committee of House and Senate members appointed to resolve differences in House and Senate versions of legislation.

CONGRESSIONAL BUDGET - The budget as set forth by Congress in a concurrent resolution on the budget. By law the resolution includes:

- the level of total budget outlays and new authority for the coming fiscal year;
- an estimate of the appropriate levels of budget outlays and new budget authority for each major functional category, for undistributed intergovernmental transactions, and for such other matters relating to the budget as may be appropriate to carry out the purpose of the 1974 Congressional Budget and Impoundment Control Act;
- the amount, if any, of the surplus or deficit in the budget;
- the recommended level of Federal receipts; and
- the appropriate level of the public debt.

CONGRESSIONAL JUSTIFICATION - The formal materials prepared by the Executive Branch presenting, explaining and defending the President's budget. The format and technical information are presented as dictated by the Clerk of the Appropriation's Subcommittee.

CONSTANT DOLLARS - A dollar value adjusted for changes in prices. Constant dollars are derived by dividing current dollar amounts by an appropriate price index, a process generally known as deflating. The result is a constant dollar series as it would presumably exist if prices and transactions were the same in all years as in the base year. Any changes in such a series would reflect only changes in the real volume of goods and services.

CONSUMER PRICE INDEX (CPI) - A measure of the price change of a fixed "market basket" of goods and service customarily purchased by consumers. The level of the CPI shows the relative cost of purchasing the specified market basket compared to the cost in a designated base year, while the rate of change in the CPI measures how fast prices are rising or falling.

CONTINGENT LIABILITY - For the purpose of Federal credit programs, a contingent liability is a conditional commitment that may become an actual liability because of a future event beyond the control of the Government. Contingent liabilities include such items as loan guarantees and bank deposit insurance.

CONTINUING RESOLUTION - Appropriations act that provides budget authority for Federal agencies and/or specific activities to continue in operation until the regular appropriations are enacted. Continuing resolutions are enacted when action on an appropriations act is not completed by the beginning of a fiscal year. The continuing resolution usually specifies a maximum rate at which the obligations may be incurred, based on the rate of the prior year, the President's budget request, or an appropriation bill passed by either or both Houses of Congress. The Congress sometimes uses a Continuing Resolution as an omnibus measure to enact a number of appropriations bills.

CONTRACT AUTHORITY - Statutory authority that permits obligations to be incurred in advance of appropriations, often in anticipation of receipts to be credited to a revolving fund or other account. (By definition, contract authority is unfunded and must subsequently be funded by an appropriation to liquidate the obligations incurred under the contract authority, or by the collection and use of receipts).

CONTROLLABLE SPENDING - The ability of Congress and the President to increase and decrease budget outlays or budget authority in the year in question, generally the current or budget year. Relatively uncontrollable refers to spending that the Federal Government cannot increase or decrease without changing existing substantive law. For example, outlays in any one year are considered to be relatively uncontrollable when the program level is determined by existing law or by contract or other obligations.

COST - The term cost, when used in connection with Federal credit programs, means the estimated long-term costs to the Government of a direct loan or loan guarantee, calculated on a net present value basis. The term excludes administrative costs and any incidental effects on governmental receipts and outlays.

COST ESTIMATES - An estimate of the 5-year cost of legislation reported by Congressional committees. The estimate is prepared by the Congressional Budget Office as required by Section 403 of the Congressional Budget Act (2 U.S.C. 639) and is published in the report accompanying the measure.

CREDIT AUTHORITY - This is authority to incur direct loan obligations and loan guarantee commitments. New credit authority must be approved in advance in an appropriations act.

CREDIT BUDGET - The levels of total new direct loan obligations, total new primary loan guarantee commitments, and total new secondary loan guarantee commitments set forth in a budget resolution. These levels form the basis for limitations on direct and guaranteed loans in appropriation bills.

CREDIT LIMIT - The limitation stated in an appropriations act on the total amount of direct or guaranteed loans that can be made in a year.

CREDIT PROGRAM ACCOUNT - An account that receives an appropriation for the cost of a direct loan or loan guarantee program, and from which such cost is disbursed to a financing account for the program when the loan or guarantee is disbursed.

CREDIT REFORM - The up-front funding of the full contingent liability of the government for subsidized credit programs.

CROSS WALK - Any procedure for expressing the relationship between budget data from one set of classifications to another, such as between appropriation accounts and authorizing legislation or between the budget functional structure and congressional jurisdictions. This term is commonly used to refer to allocations made pursuant to Section 302 of the Congressional Budget Act.

CURRENT DOLLARS - The value of goods and services in dollar costs experienced in that year.

CURRENT POLICY - An estimate of the budget authority and outlays required to continue existing programs in the next or future fiscal years based on its priority within the President's Total Budget Estimate. Programs whose spending is fixed in law would not be adjusted for inflation. Other Programs may be increased, reduced, or remain constant reflecting the President's Priorities.

CURRENT YEAR - Fiscal year for which funds are being obligated and expended.

CURRENT SERVICES ESTIMATES - Presidential estimates of budget authority and outlays for future fiscal years based on continuation of existing levels of service. These estimates reflect the anticipated effects of inflation on the cost of continuing Federal programs and activities at present spending levels without policy changes. The estimates do not assume any new initiatives, Presidential or Congressional, that are not yet law. (See Budget Baseline.)

These estimates of budget authority and outlays, accompanied by the underlying economic and programmatic assumptions upon which they are based (such as the rate of inflation, the rate of economic growth, the unemployment rate, program caseloads, and pay increases) are required to be transmitted by the President to the Congress with the President's budget. CBO produces a baseline used by the Congress.

DEBT - Amounts borrowed by the Treasury or the Federal Financing Bank (public debt) or by any other agency of the U.S. Government (agency debt). Most agency debt is excluded from the statutory limit on the public debt.

DEBT HELD BY THE GOVERNMENT - Holdings of Federal Trust Funds and other special government funds. Surplus funds in Federal Trust Funds, such as the Old Age and Disability Retirement Trust Fund, are invested in government securities.

DEBT HELD BY THE PUBLIC - Value of Federal debt held by individuals, institutions, and others outside the Federal government.

DEBT MANAGEMENT - The operations of the U.S. Treasury Department that determine the composition of the Federal debt. Debt management involves determining the amounts, maturities, other terms and conditions, and schedule of offerings of Federal debt securities and raising new cash to finance the Government's operations at least cost to the taxpayer and in a manner that will minimize the effect of Government operations on financial markets and on the economy.

DEFERRAL OF BUDGET AUTHORITY - Any action or inaction by an officer or employee of the United States Government that temporarily withholds, delays, or effectively precludes the obligation or expenditure of budget authority, including authority to obligate by contract in advance of appropriations as specifically authorized by law. Pursuant to the Congressional Budget and Impoundment Control Act 1974, the President must provide advance notice to the Congress on proposed deferrals.

DEFICIENCY APPORTIONMENT - A distribution by the Office of Management and Budget of available budgetary resources for the fiscal year that anticipates the need for supplemental budget authority. Such apportionments may only be made under certain specified conditions provided for in law (Antideficiency Act, 31 U.S.C. 665 (e)). In such instances, the need for additional budget authority is usually reflected by making the amount apportioned for the fourth quarter less than the amount that will actually be required. Approval of requests for deficiency apportionment does not authorize agencies to exceed available resources within an account.

DEFICIENCY APPROPRIATION - An appropriation made to an expired account to cover obligations that have been incurred in excess of available funds. Deficiency appropriations are rare since obligating in excess of available funds generally is prohibited by law. Deficiency appropriation is sometimes erroneously used as a synonym for supplemental appropriation.

DEFICIT - The amount by which outlays exceed Governmental receipts in a given fiscal year.

DEFICIT FINANCING - A situation in which the Federal Government's excess of outlays over receipts for a given period is financed primarily by borrowing from the public.

DEFINITE AUTHORITY - Authority which is stated as a specific sum at the time the authority is granted. This includes authority stated as "not to exceed" a specified amount.

DEPARTMENTAL - SEE AGENCY.

DIRECT LOAN - A disbursement of funds under a contract that requires repayment with or without interest. It includes direct Federal participation in loans privately made or held and purchase of private loans through secondary market operations.

For informational purposes, transactions similar to direct loans are sometimes displayed in the budget, e.g., the sale of Federal assets on credit terms for more than 90 days duration; investments in obligations or preferred stock of any privately owned enterprises; and deferred or delinquent interest that is capitalized.

DIRECT SPENDING - Direct spending, also known as mandatory spending, consists of entitlement authority, the budget authority for the food stamp program, and budget authority provided in law other than annual appropriations acts.

DISBURSEMENT - Cash expenditure.

DISCRETIONARY APPROPRIATIONS - A category of budget authority that comprises budget authority and budgetary resources (except those provided to fund direct-spending programs) provided in appropriations acts.

DISCRETIONARY SPENDING - A category of spending (budget authority and outlays) subject to annual appropriations.

DISINVESTMENT - A term that is sometimes used to refer to the status of national physical infrastructure. Disinvestment occurs when the rate of deterioration of physical infrastructure exceeds the rate on new investment in rehabilitation and improvements in infrastructure.

ECONOMIC INDICATORS - A set of statistical series that have had a systematic relationship to the business cycle. Each indicator is classified as leading, coincident, or lagging, depending on whether the indicator generally changes direction in advance or, coincident with, or subsequent to changes in the overall economy.

EMERGENCY APPROPRIATION - An appropriation in a discretionary category that the President and the Congress have designated as an emergency requirement. Such appropriations result in an adjustment to the Budget Enforcement Act cap for the category.

EMERGENCY SPENDING - Emergency spending is spending that the President and the Congress have designated as an emergency requirement. Such spending is not subject to the limits on discretionary spending, if it is discretionary spending, or the pay-as-you-go rules, if it is direct spending.

ENROLLED BILL - Final Bill transmitted to the President for approval or disapproval.

ENROLLED BILL MEMO - Memorandum to the President recommending approval or disapproval of spending authority by the Agency's staff through OMB. Requires sign off by the Cabinet officer prior to presentation to the President.

ENTITLEMENT AUTHORITY - Legislation that requires the payment of benefits (or entitlement) to any person or unit of government that meets the eligibility requirements established by such law. Budget authority for such payments is usually provided by authorization legislation and constitutes direct (or monthly) spending otherwise, entitlement legislation requires the subsequent enactment of appropriations unless the existing appropriation is permanent. Examples of entitlement programs are social security benefits, veterans' compensation or pensions.

EXPENDITURE - Generally the same as an outlay, or a cash payment to settle an obligation.

FEDERAL FUNDS - The moneys collected and spent by the Government other than those designated as trust funds. Federal funds include general, special, public enterprise, and intra-governmental funds.

FINANCING ACCOUNT - An account that receives the cost payments from a credit program account and includes all cash flows to and from the Government resulting from direct loan obligations or loan guarantee commitments beginning in FY 1992. At least one financing account is associated with each credit program account. For programs with direct and guaranteed loans, there are separate financing accounts for direct loans and guaranteed loans. The transactions of the financing accounts are not included in the budget totals.

FISCAL POLICY - Federal Government policies with respect to taxes, spending, and debt management, intended to promote the nation's macroeconomic goals, particularly with respect to employment, gross national product, price level stability, and equilibrium in the balance of payments. The budget process is a major vehicle for determining and implementing Federal fiscal policy. The other major component of Federal macroeconomic policy is monetary policy.

FISCAL YEAR - The Government's accounting period. It begins on October 1st and ends on September 30th, and is designated by the calendar year in which it ends.

FULL FUNDING - Provides budgetary resources to cover the total cost of a program or project at the time it is undertaken. Full funding differs from incremental funding, where budget authority is provided or recorded for only a portion of total estimated obligations expected to be incurred during a single fiscal year. Full funding is generally discussed in terms of multi-year programs, whether or not obligations for the entire program are made in the first year.

FUNCTIONAL CLASSIFICATION - A classification of budget resources that permits all budget authority, outlays, loan guarantees, and tax expenditures to be related in terms of the national needs being addressed.

Appropriation accounts are generally placed in the single budget function (e.g., National Defense, Health) that best reflects its major end purpose. A function may be divided into two or more subfunctions, depending upon the complexity of the national need addressed by that function. There are 19 functional categories of national need and one category for undistributed offsetting receipts.

FUND ACCOUNTING - The legal requirement for Federal agencies to establish accounts for segregating revenues and other resources, together with all related liabilities, obligations, and reserves, for the purpose of carrying on specific activities or attaining certain objectives in accordance with special regulations, restrictions, or limitations. Fund accounting, in a broad sense, is required in the Federal Government to demonstrate agency compliance with requirements of existing legislation for which Federal funds have been appropriated or otherwise authorized.

GENERAL FUND - The account for receipts not earmarked by law for a specific purpose, the proceeds of general borrowing, and the expenditure of these moneys.

GENERAL PROVISIONS - Directives and instructions that Congress includes in an Appropriations Act.

GOVERNMENTAL RECEIPTS - Collections from the public that result primarily from the Government's exercise of its sovereign power to tax or otherwise compel payment. They include individual and corporation income taxes, social insurance taxes, excise taxes, compulsory user charges, customs duties, court fines, certain license fees, and deposits of earnings of the Federal Reserve System. They are compared to outlays in calculating a surplus or deficit.

GOVERNMENT SPONSORED ENTERPRISES - Enterprises established and chartered by the Federal Government to perform specific functions under the supervision of a Government agency. Since they are private corporations, they are excluded from the budget totals. However, an analysis of the financial condition of Government Sponsored Enterprises and Federal risk exposure from their activities are presented in the Budget of the United States Government.

GRANTS - Assistance awards in which substantial involvement is not anticipated between the Federal Government and the State or local government or other recipient during the performance of the contemplated activity. Such assistance is not limited to a State or local government as in the case of grants-in-aid.

The two major forms of Federal grants are block and categorical.

- Block grants are given primarily to general purpose governmental units in accordance with a statutory formula. Formula grants allocate Federal funds to States or their subdivisions in accordance with a distribution formula prescribed by law or administrative regulation. Such grants can be used for a variety of activities within a broad functional area. Community Development Block Grants are an example.

- Categorical grants are formula, project, and formula-project grants that can be used only for a specific program and are usually limited to narrowly defined activities.

GROSS DOMESTIC PRODUCT (GDP) - The total value of all goods and services produced by labor and property supplied by residents of the United States in a given period of time. Depreciation charges and other allowances for business and institutional consumption of fixed capital goods are subtracted from GDP to derive Net National Product (NNP). GDP comprises the purchases of all final goods and services by persons and governments, gross private domestic investment (including the change in business inventories), and net exports (exports less imports). Government Expenditures are assumed to have a value identical to the expenditure. GDP can be expressed in current or constant dollars.

IDENTIFICATION CODES - Each appropriation or fund account in The Budget of the United States Government carries an 11-digit code that identifies: (a) the agency, (b) the account, (c) the timing of the transmittal to Congress, (d) the type of fund, and (e) the account's functional classification.

IMPOUNDMENT - Any action or inaction by an officer or employee of the United States Government that precludes the obligation of budget authority provided by Congress.

INCREMENTAL FUNDING - The provision of budget resources for an investment program or project that covers only the obligations that will be incurred during one fiscal year of a program spanning several years. This differs from full funding, where budget resources are provided for the total estimated obligations for a program or project in the initial year of funding.

INDEFINITE AUTHORITY - Authority for which a specific sum is not stated but is determined by other factors, such as, the receipts from a certain source or obligations incurred. (Authority to borrow that is limited to a specified amount that may be outstanding at any time, i.e., revolving debt authority is considered to be indefinite budget authority).

INFORMAL HEARING - Discussions between Congressional members and political appointees.

INTRA-GOVERNMENTAL FUNDS - Accounts for business-type or market-oriented activities conducted primarily within and between Government agencies and financed by offsetting collections that are credited directly to the fund.

INVESTMENT INITIATIVES - A term that is used to describe proposed budget increases for federal programs that support infrastructure, technology, skills, and security – all of which yield public benefits far into the future.

LINE ITEM - In executive budgeting, the term usually refers to a particular item or expenditure such as travel costs or equipment. In congressional budgeting, it refers to particular accounts or programs assumed in the budget aggregates, functional allocations, or reconciliation instructions. Although line items are not specified in congressional budget resolutions, the aggregate functional classifications and reconciliation instructions reflect assumptions about such items. A line item may be a specific directive by Congress to set-aside spending for a specific purpose within the total appropriation account structure.

LIQUIDATING ACCOUNT - An account that includes all cash flows to and from the Government resulting from direct loan obligations and loan guarantee commitments made prior to FY 1992.

LIQUIDATING APPROPRIATION - An appropriation to pay obligations incurred pursuant to substantive legislation, usually contract authority. A liquidating appropriation is not regarded as budget authority.

LOAN GUARANTEE - An agreement by which the Government agrees to pay part or all of the loan principal and interest of a non-Federal borrower to a non-Federal lender or holder of a security, in the event of default by a third party borrower.

MANAGEMENT AGENDA - Initiatives proposed within the Executive Branch to improve overall program/project efficiency. This includes implementation of the recommendations of the National Performance Review on Reinventing Government.

MANDATORY SPENDING - Spending authority from mandatory programs. Used synonymously with direct spending.

MARK-UP - This is a meeting at which a Congressional Committee works on the language of a specific bill or piece of legislation.

MAXIMUM DEFICIT AMOUNTS - Amounts specified in and subject to certain adjustments under law. If the deficit for the year in question is estimated to exceed the adjusted maximum deficit amount for that year by more than a specified margin, a sequester of the excess deficit is required.

MEANS OF FINANCING - Ways in which a budget deficit is financed or a budget surplus is used. A budget deficit may be financed by Treasury (or agency) borrowing, by reducing Treasury cash balances, by allowing unpaid liabilities to increase, or by certain equivalent transactions. Conversely, a budget surplus may be used to repay borrowing or to build up cash balances.

MONETARY POLICY - Policies which affect the money supply interest rates and credit availability that are intended to promote national macroeconomic goals, such as price stability and full employment. Particular significance is assigned to employment, gross national product, price stability, and equilibrium in the balance of payments in policy development. Monetary policy is directed primarily by the Board of Governors of the Federal Reserve System and the Federal Open Market Committee. Monetary policy works by influencing the cost and availability of bank reserves.

MONTHLY TREASURY STATEMENT - A summary statement prepared from agency accounting reports and issued by the Department of Treasury. The MTS presents the receipts, outlays, and resulting budget surplus or deficit for the month and the fiscal year to date.

MULTI-YEAR APPROPRIATION - Budget authority that is available for a specified period of time in excess of one fiscal year. This authority may cover periods that do not coincide with the start or end of a fiscal year.

MULTI-YEAR BUDGET PLANNING - A budget planning process designed to make sure that the long-range consequences of budget decisions are identified and reflected in the budget totals. This process provides a structure for the review and analysis of long-term program and tax policy choices.

NATIONAL INCOME ACCOUNTS - Accounts prepared and published quarterly and annually by the Department of Commerce, which provide a detailed statistical description of aggregate economic activity within the U.S. economy. These accounts depict in dollar terms the composition and use of the nation's output and the distribution of nation income to different recipients. The accounts make it possible to trace fluctuations in economic activity.

NONEXPENDITURE TRANSACTIONS - Intra-governmental transactions between appropriation and fund accounts that do not represent payments for goods and services received or to be received but serve only to adjust the amounts available in the accounts for making payments. Nonexpenditure transactions are not recorded as obligations or outlays of the transferring accounts or as reimbursements or as collections of the receiving accounts. The statutory restrictions on the purpose, availability, and use of appropriated funds by administrative agencies require that no change be made in the availability of funds by agencies through the use of nonexpenditure transactions unless specifically authorized by law.

OBJECT CLASSIFICATION - A uniform classification identifying the transactions of the Federal Government by the nature of the goods or services purchased (such as personnel compensation, supplies and materials, and equipment). Data on obligations by object classification are provided in the Object Classification Schedule along with the corresponding Program and Financing Schedule in the Budget of the United States Government.

OBLIGATED BALANCES - Amounts of budget authority that have been obligated but not yet outlayed. Unobligated balances are amounts that have not been obligated and that remain available for obligation under law.

OBLIGATIONS - Binding agreements that will result in outlays, immediately or in the future. Budgetary resources must be available before obligations can be incurred legally.

OBLIGATIONAL AUTHORITY - The sum of (a) budget authority provided for a given fiscal year, (b) balances of amounts brought forward from prior years that remain available for obligation, and (c) amounts authorized to be credited to a specific fund or account during that year, including transfers between funds or accounts.

OBLIGATION-BASED BUDGETING - Financial transactions that record obligations when they are incurred, regardless of when the resources acquired are to be consumed.

OBLIGATION LIMITATION - This term generally refers to limitations in appropriations acts on the amount of offsetting collections that can be counted as budget authority. In the absence of such a limitation, the whole amount of the offsetting collection would be counted as budget authority.

OBLIGATIONS INCURRED - Amounts of orders placed, contracts awarded, services received, and similar transactions during a given period that will require payments during the same or a future period. Such amounts include outlays for which obligations had not been previously recorded and reflect adjustments for differences between obligations previously recorded and actual outlays to liquidate those obligations.

OFF-BUDGET - Transactions that are excluded from the budget totals under law, even though these outlays are part of total Government spending. Current law requires that Social Security trust funds and the Postal Service be off-budget.

OFFSETTING COLLECTIONS - Collections from the public that result from business-type or market-oriented activities and collections from other Government accounts. These collections are deducted from gross disbursements in calculating outlays, rather than counted in Governmental receipt totals. Some are credited directly to appropriation or fund accounts; others, called offsetting receipts, are credited to receipt accounts. The authority to spend offsetting collections is a form of budget authority.

OFFSETTING RECEIPTS - Amounts deposited in receipt accounts (i.e., general funds, special funds, or trust funds). These receipts generally are deducted from budget authority and outlays by function and/or subfunction, and by agency. Offsetting receipts are subdivided between proprietary receipts from the public and intra-governmental transactions. These receipts do not offset budget authority and outlays at the appropriations account level.

OMB HEARINGS - Presentation and justification of the Department's budget submission to OMB.

OMB PASSBACK   -   Process for notifying Executive Branch Departments/Agencies of OMB's decisions on the Budget for the next fiscal year. Under the reinventing Government initiative, this process has been replaced by a more informal discussion process between OMB and the Agencies.

ON-BUDGET - The total of all transactions for all federal government entities except those excluded from the budget totals by law.

ONE-YEAR (ANNUAL) AUTHORITY - Budget authority that is available for obligation only during a specified fiscal year and expires at the end of that time.

OUTCOME - The results of a government program.

OUTLAY RATES - The rate at which budget authority is expended. It is expressed as a percentage of the available budget authority that will be expended in the current year and in each subsequent year.

OUTLAYS - Measure of government spending. Outlays are payments to liquidate obligations (other than repayment of debt), net of refunds and offsetting collections. Outlays are generally recorded on a cash basis, but they also include cash-equivalent transactions, the subsidy cost of direct loans and loan guarantees, and interest accrued on public issues of Treasury debt. Outlays during a fiscal year may be for payment of obligations incurred in prior years (prior-year outlays) or in the same year. The terms expenditure and net disbursement are frequently used interchangeably with the term outlays.

OUTPUT - A level of program activity or effort expressed in a quantitative or qualitative manner.

OUTYEARS - A year (or years) beyond the budget year for which projections are made.

PASSBACK - Generally refers to decisions by the Director on OMB with the concurrence of the President on an Agency's total budget level as well as individual program and policy decision.

PAY-AS-YOU-GO - Requirement established in the Budget Enforcement Act that requires new direct (mandatory) spending increases or tax reductions in legislation to be offset by legislated reductions in other mandatory spending or by revenue increases. A sequester if the estimated combined result of legislation affecting direct spending or receipts is an increase in the deficit for a fiscal year.

PERFORMANCE GOAL - a target level of performance expressed in measurable terms (standard, value, or rate) that permits comparison with actual achievement.

PERFORMANCE INDICATOR - A particular value or characteristic used to measure output or outcome. This is a key element in reporting under the Government Results and Performance Act.

PERMANENT APPROPRIATION - Budget authority that becomes available as the result of previously enacted legislation (substantive legislation or prior appropriation act) and does not require current action by Congress. Authority created by such legislation is considered to be "current" if provided in the current session of Congress and "permanent" if provided in prior sessions.

PERMANENT AUTHORIZATION - An authorization without limit of time and, usually, without limit of money. A permanent authorization continues in effect unless changed or terminated by Congress.

POCKET VETO - Presidential failure to sign an enrolled bill following the end of the Congressional session.

POINT OF ORDER - Motion in order on both the House and Senate Floors when spending authority either violates the cap or is not within authorized limits.

PORK BARREL PROJECTS - Low priority, special interest funding sponsored by individual Congressional members.

PRESIDENTIAL APPEAL - Departmental appeals of OMB Passback decisions to the President when appeals to OMB have not been resolved to the satisfaction of the department or agency head.

PRESIDENT'S BUDGET - The document sent to Congress by the President no later than the first Monday in February in accordance with the Budget Enforcement Act. It sets forth the President's comprehensive financial plan and indicates the President's policy/program priorities and proposed spending levels for the Federal Government.

PRESIDENT'S BUDGET PRESS RELEASE - The Director of OMB, the Chairman of the Council Economic Advisors, and the Secretary of the Treasury prepare a coordinated press release highlighting significant measures included in the President's proposals to Congress. They also conduct a press conference but embargo the information until the President's Announcement.

PROGRAM - Generally defined as an organized set of activities directed toward a common purpose, or goal, undertaken or proposed by an agency in order to carry out its responsibilities. In practice, however, the term program has many uses and thus does not have a well-defined, standard meaning in the legislative process. Program is used to describe an agency's mission, programs, functions, activities, services, projects, and processes.

PROGRAM ACTIVITY - A specific activity or project listed in the program and financing schedules of the annual budget of the United States Government. Under the Government Performance and Results Act, performance goals and indicators are to be developed for program activities.

PROGRAM AND FINANCING SCHEDULE - A schedule, published in the Appendix to The Budget of the United States, presenting detailed budget data. The schedule consists of three sections: (1) Program by Activities; (2) Financing; and (3) Relation of Obligations to Outlays.

PROGRAM EVALUATION - In general, the process of assessing program alternatives, including research and results, and the options for meeting program objectives and future expectations. Specifically, program evaluation is the process of appraising the manner and extent to which programs:

- achieve their stated objectives,
- meet the performance perceptions and expectations of responsible Federal officials and other interested groups, and
- produce other significant effects of either a desirable or undesirable character.

PROPRIETARY RECEIPTS FROM THE PUBLIC - These are collections from the public, deposited in receipt accounts, that arise from market-oriented or business-type activities of the Federal government.

PUBLIC ENTERPRISE FUNDS - Revolving accounts authorized by Congress to be credited with collections, primarily from the public, that are generated by, and earmarked to finance a continuing cycle of business-type operations.

QUESTIONS & ANSWERS - Written responses not included in the Hearing record provided mainly for Congressional staff analysis.

QUESTIONS & ANSWERS (AS IF ASKED) - Written responses to be included in the Congressional Hearing record subsequent to direct testimony.

REAPPORTIONMENT - A revision by OMB to a previous apportionment of budgetary resources for an appropriation or fund account. Agency requests for reapportionment are usually submitted to OMB as soon as a change in previous apportionment becomes necessary due to changes in amounts available, program requirements, or cost factors.

REAPPROPRIATIONS - Congressional action to continue the obligational availability, whether for the same or different purposes, of all or part of the unobligated portion of budget authority that has expired or would otherwise expire. Reappropriations are counted as budget authority in the year for which the availability is newly available.

RECEIPTS - Collections that result primarily from the Government's exercise of its sovereign power to tax or otherwise compel payment. Receipts are compared to outlays in calculating a surplus or deficit.

RECESSION - A decline in overall business activity that is pervasive, substantial, and of at least several months duration. Historically, recessions have been identified by a decline in real gross national product for at least two consecutive quarters.

RECONCILIATION - A process used by Congress to reconcile spending amounts contained in tax, spending, and debt legislation for a given fiscal year with the ceilings in the concurrent resolution for that year. The Congressional Budget and Impoundment Control Act of 1974 (2 U.S.C. 641) provides that the resolution on the budget, which sets binding totals for the budget, may direct committees to determine and recommend changes to laws, bills, and resolutions, as required to conform with the resolution's binding totals for budget authority, revenues, and the public debt. Such changes are incorporated into a reconciliation bill. Changes in tax laws are generally contained in a separate bill.

RE-ESTIMATES - Changes made in executive or congressional budget estimates due to changes in economic conditions, spendout rates, workload, and other factors but not to changes in policy. From time to time, the re-estimates are entered into the scorekeeping system.

REFUNDABLE TAX CREDITS - Certain tax credits are refundable to the taxpayer. If the credit is refundable, the amount of the credit in excess of tax liability is paid to the taxpayer. An example is the Earned Income Tax Credit.

REGULATORY AGENDA - Projected list of regulations under development within the Executive Branch pursuant to substantive law.

REIMBURSEMENTS - Sums received by an agency as a payment for or services furnished either to the public or to another Government account. They are authorized by law to be credited directly to specific appropriation and fund accounts. These amounts are deducted from the total obligations incurred (and outlays) in determining net obligations (and outlays) for such accounts.

REINVENTING GOVERNMENT - A term used to refer to the National Performance Review, a process under the direction of Vice President Al Gore. Reinventing Government generally means challenging basic assumptions and methods for implementing government programs. The objective of reinventing government is to change the way government works in order to make it work better and cost less.

REPORT LANGUAGE - Statement of Congressional policy included in the report accompanying a bill but not included in the statute. It is advisory to the Executive Branch.

REPROGRAMMING - Use of funds in an appropriation account for purposes other than those contemplated at the time of appropriation. Reprogramming is generally preceded by consultation between the Federal agencies and the appropriate Congressional committees. It involves formal notification and, in some instances, opportunity for disapproval by Congressional committees.

RESCISSION - Cancellation of budget authority provided in an appropriations act before it would otherwise lapse (i.e. funds cease to be available for obligation).

The Congressional Budget and Impoundment Control Act of 1974 (P.L. 93-344; 2 U.S.C. 683) specifies that whenever the President determines that all or part of any budget authority will not be needed to carry out the full objectives or scope of programs for which the authority was provided, the President will propose to Congress that the excess funds be rescinded. Budget authority may also be proposed for rescission for fiscal policy or other reasons. Generally, amounts proposed for rescission are withheld for up to 45 legislative days while the proposals are being considered by Congress. All funds proposed for rescission, including those withheld, must be reported to Congress in a special message. If both Houses have not approved action on a rescission proposed by the President within 45 calendar days of continuous session, any funds being withheld must be made available for obligation.

RESOURCE MANAGEMENT OFFICES (RMOs) - Offices within the Office of Management and Budget responsible for developing the budget and implementing management and policy reforms for assigned areas. These offices are headed by Program Associate Directors, known as PADs. There are five RMOs – Natural Resources, Energy and Science; National Security and International Affairs; Health and Personnel; Human Resources, and General Government.

REVOLVING FUNDS - Funds for business-type activities in which collections are used to pay for goods and services produced. There are three types of revolving funds – public enterprise, intra-governmental, and trust revolving. The budget reflects the net of collections and outlays.

SCOREKEEPING - Procedures for tracking the status of Congressional budget actions. Examples of scorekeeping information include up-to-date tabulations and reports on Congressional actions affecting budget authority, receipts, outlays, surplus or deficit, and the public debt limit. Scorekeeping generally compares the spending or receipts caused by legislation with a baseline, such as the budget resolution, the President's budget, or the current services baselines.

Both CBO and OMB have statutory scorekeeping responsibilities. Scorekeeping data published by the CBO include, but are not limited to, status reports on the effects of congressional actions (and in the case of scorekeeping reports prepared for the Senate Budget Committee, the budget effects of potential congressional actions), and comparisons of these actions to targets and ceilings set by Congress in the budget resolutions. Periodic scorekeeping reports from CBO are required by section 308(b) of the Congressional Budget and Impoundment Control Act of 1974 (P.L. 93-344, 2 U.S.C. 602).

The OMB is required by the Budget Enforcement Act to provide Congress with estimated costs of legislation within five days of its enactment, including comparisons with discretionary spending caps and pay-as-you-go impact on mandatory spending.

SECRETARIAL APPEAL - Program or bureau appeals of the Department's budget formulation decisions to the Secretary.

SEQUESTER - The automatic cancellation of budgetary resources provided by discretionary appropriations or direct spending legislation, following procedures prescribed in law. A sequester may occur in response to a breach of the discretionary budget authority or outlay limits, an increase in the deficit resulting from the combined result of legislation affecting direct spending or receipts (referred to as a "pay-as-you-go" sequester), or a deficit estimated to be in excess of the maximum allowable deficit amount.

SPECIAL FUNDS - Accounts for receipts earmarked for specific purposes and the associated expenditure of those receipts.

SPENDING AUTHORITY - As defined by the Congressional Budget and Impoundment Control Act of 1974 (P.L. 93-344, 31 U.S.C. 1323), a collective designation for appropriations, borrowing authority, contract authority, and other authority for which the budget authority is not provided in advance by appropriation acts. The latter three are also referred to as backdoor authority.

SPENDING CAPS - Specific discretionary spending ceilings for federal programs. Currently, the caps extend through 2002. For FY 2000, the specific categories are (1) violent crime reduction, (2) highways, (3) mass transit, and (4) other, including national defense. The cap on violent crime reduction is eliminated in FY 2001.

SPEND-OUT RATE - Rate at which budget authority is expended. (See Outlay Rates)

SPRING PLANNING REVIEW - OMB Functional and Program specific reviews to establish presidential policy for the upcoming budget.

STATUTORY LIMITATION ON THE PUBLIC DEBT - The maximum amount of public debt that can be outstanding. The limit covers virtually all public debt, including intra-governmental borrowing from trust funds and debt of off-budget entities.

STRATEGIC PLAN - A comprehensive statement of an agency's mission, general goals and objectives, and the resources needed to achieve the goals. It is a key document required by the Government Performance and Results Act.

SUBCOMMITTEE\COMMITTEE MARK UP - Meeting of members of a Congressional Committee and staff to change the President's budget proposal.

SUBSIDY - Subsidies are designed to support the conduct of an economic enterprise or activity, such as ship operations. They may also refer to provisions of loans, goods, and services to the public at prices lower than market value, such as interest subsidies. Under credit reform accounting, the subsidy is the present value of unreimbursed outlays by federal direct and guaranteed loan programs. Subsidy cost became the budget authority measure for loans beginning in FY 1992.

SUBSTANTIVE LAW - Statutory public law other than an appropriation act; sometimes referred to as basic law. Substantive law usually authorizes, in broad general terms, the executive branch to carry out a program of work. Annual determination of the amount of the work to be done is usually embodied in appropriation acts, except for entitlements, which direct spending authority usually is provided in substantive law.

SUPER MAJORITY - The required sixty-five Senate votes to override a breach of the discretionary spending cap or certain points of order defined in the Budget Enforcement Act.

SUPPLEMENTALS - New appropriations enacted after an annual appropriations bill has been enacted when the need for funds is too urgent to be postponed until the next regular annual appropriations act. Under the current Budget Enforcement Act, supplemental funding is possible only if: (1) the cap for that category of funding has not been exceeded; (2) an offset is included in the supplemental; or (3) the President and Congress agree that the supplemental is a dire emergency and therefore not subject to the cap.

SURPLUS - The amount by which receipts exceed outlays.

TAX EXPENDITURES - Subsidy in the form of a tax law that allows an exclusion, exemption or deduction from gross income or provides a credit or deferral of tax liability with the result that the federal government forgoes revenue that would have otherwise accrued to it.

TRANSFER BETWEEN APPROPRIATION/FUND ACCOUNTS - A transaction that, pursuant to law, withdraws budget authority or balances from one appropriation account for credit to another appropriations account.

Withdrawals that are adjustments to obligatory authority are treated as "adjustments of budgetary resources" rather than as payments. Payments to other accounts for goods or services are not transfers but are outlay (expenditure) transactions.

TRANSFER PAYMENTS - In the national income accounts, payments made by the Federal Government or business firms to individuals or organizations for which no current or future goods or services are required to be provided in return. Government transfer payments include social security benefits, unemployment insurance benefits, retirement and veterans' benefits, and welfare payments. Transfer payments by business firms consist mainly of gifts to nonprofit institutions.

TRANSFER OF FUNDS - When specifically authorized in law, all or part of the budget authority in one account may be transferred to another account.

TRUST FUNDS - Accounts, designated by law as trust funds, for receipts earmarked for specific purposes and the associated expenditure of those receipts.

UNDISTRIBUTED OFFSETTING RECEIPTS - The receipts that are deducted from government wide totals for budget authority and outlays. An example is the collection of rents and royalties on the Outer Continental Shelf lands. Undistributed offsetting receipts are included as a separate category in the Functional Classification.

UNFUNDED FEDERAL MANDATES - Any provision in legislation, a statute, or a regulation that would impose an enforceable duty on state, local, or tribal government, or the private sector, except as a condition for participation in a voluntary Federal program. Exceptions are enforcing constitutional rights, statutory provisions against discrimination, emergency assistance requested by states, accounting or auditing for Federal assistance, national security, Presidentially designated emergencies, and Social Security.

UNIFIED BUDGET - The present form of the budget of the Federal Government adopted beginning with the 1969 budget, in which receipts and outlays from Federal funds and trust funds are consolidated. When these fund groups are consolidated to display budget totals, transactions that are outlays of one fund group for payment to the other fund group (i.e., intra-governmental transactions) are deducted to avoid double counting. By law, budget authority and outlays of off-budget entities are excluded from certain estimates in the President's Budget and the Concurrent Resolution on the Budget. Data relating to off-budget entities are displayed in the budget documents.

UNOBLIGATED BALANCES - The portion of budget authority that has not yet been obligated.

USER FEES - Fees, charges, and assessments levied on the people or organizations directly benefitting from or subject to regulation by government programs or activities, that are used solely to support the program or activity.

VETO - Presidential disapproval of an enrolled bill.

WARRANTS - Documents issued by the Secretary of the Treasury that establish the amount of money authorized to be withdrawn from the Treasury.

Key Laws Affecting the Budget Process

Anti-Defiency Act

- This makes it a criminal offense for an officer or employee of the United States Government or the District of Columbia government to make or authorize an expenditure or obligation that exceeds available funds.

Constitution

- This requires appropriations in law before money may be spent from the Treasury, and that revenue legislation be initiated in the House of Representatives.

Budget and Accounting Act of 1921 (P.L. 67-13)

- Bureau of the Budget (later Office of Management and Budget) was created to assist President in preparing budget recommendations for submission to Congress

- General Accounting Office (GAO) was created as principal auditing arm of the Federal government

Congressional Budget and Impoundment Control Act of 1974 (P.L. 93-344)

- Congressional Budget Act of 1974 prescribes the congressional budget process and created the Congressional Budget Office, and

- Impoundment Control Act of 1974 controls certain aspects of budget execution.

Balanced Budget and Emergency Deficit Control of 1985 commonly known as Gramm-Rudman-Hollings. (P.L. 99-177)

- Annual deficit targets were set leading to a balanced budget by 1991 and a sequester process was created to eliminate excess spending.
- The act was modified in 1987 and the annual deficit targets were adjusted to achieve a balanced budget by 1993. (P.L. 100-119)

Budget Enforcement Act of 1990 (Title XIII, P.L. 101-508)

- This amended the Congressional Budget Act and the Balanced Budget and Emergency Deficit Control Act.
- Limits or caps were set on level of discretionary appropriations for fiscal years 1991 through 1995, PAYGO rule for mandatory spending and receipts was created, and sequester process was expanded to remove excess if discretionary or mandatory spending exceeded the new limits.
- The BEA includes the Federal Credit Reform Act of 1990, which prescribes budget treatment for Federal credit programs.

Omnibus Budget Reconciliation Act of 1993 (P.L. 103-66)

- The discretionary caps were extended through FY 1998.

Government Performance and Results Act of 1993 (P.L. 103-62)

- This requires reports on performance of government programs.
- Performance data is to be provided for all major programs in the FY 1999 budget.

Line Item Veto Act (P.L. 104-130)

- This gives the President the authority to cancel line items in appropriations and tax acts. It was ruled unconstitutional by the United States Supreme Court in 1998.

Budget Enforcement Act of 1997 (P.L. 105-33)

- The discretionary caps were set through FY 2002.

About the EOP Foundation and the Author

The EOP Foundation was formed to promote efficient human resources management, cost/beneficial environmental and natural resources management, improved science and technology policy, and innovative policy regarding Native Americans. In carrying out these objectives, the Foundation conducts a broad range of activities, including analytical studies, research, and executive development and training. Included in this diverse range of activities are Executive Training and Development programs for the Federal Government and assistance in creating an automobile mechanical training center targeted for Washington-area youth.

The Foundation's officers are former senior-level budget officials from the White House Office of Management and Budget (OMB).

The primary author responsible for this book is Donald Gessaman. Mr. Gessaman began working for the Federal Government in 1963 as a program analyst for the U.S. Air Force. After an assignment in the Office of the Secretary of Defense, he joined the staff of OMB where he worked for 28 years. He was Deputy Associate Director for National Security Programs when he retired in 1995. Mr. Gessaman received the Presidential awards of Meritorious Executive and Distinguished Executive, as well as the Distinguished Public Service Medal from the Secretary of Defense. In June of 1995, Mr. Gessaman joined the EOP Group and EOP Foundation as a Senior Consultant.

The principals of the Foundation, Messrs. Michael J. O'Bannon and Joseph S. Hezir, also played a major role in the preparation of this book. Overall, they have a total of almost 50 years of experience at the highest levels of budget formulation in the Federal Government, including work at OMB.

Mr. O'Bannon worked at OMB from 1976 through 1980. After that he served in a variety of positions involved with budget and financial matters at the Department of Interior and at the Export-Import Bank until 1988. Since then, he has been providing consulting services to firms dealing with the Federal Government.

Mr. Hezir served for eighteen years in OMB. When he left in 1992, he was Deputy Associate Director for Energy and Science, with oversight responsibility for the Department of Energy, the National Aeronautics and Space Administration, the National Science Foundation, and other agencies with science and energy responsibilities.

NOTES

NOTES

NOTES

NOTES

NOTES